EDITORIAL

Can't say; won't say

Vital moments during our lifetimes are complicated by taboos about what we can and can't talk about, and we end up making the wrong decisions just because we don't get the full picture, says **Rachael Jolley**

47(04): 1/3 | DOI: 10.1177/0306422018819303

BIRTH, MARRIAGE AND death – these are key staging posts. And that's one reason why this issue looks at how taboos around these subjects have a critical impact on our world.

Sadly, there are still many of us who feel we can't talk about problems openly at these times. Societal pressure to conform can be a powerful element in this and can help to create stultifying silences that frighten us into not being able to speak.

Being unable to discuss something that has a major and often complex impact on you or your family can lead to ignorance, fear and terrible decisions.

Not knowing about information or medical advice can also mean exposing people to illness and even death.

The Australian Museum sees death as the last taboo, but it also traces where those ideas

have come from and how we are sometimes more shy to talk about subjects now than we were in the past.

The Sydney-based museum's research considers how different cultures have disposed of the dead throughout history and where the concepts of cemeteries and burials have come from.

For instance, in Ancient Rome, only those of very high status were buried within the city walls, while the Ancient Greeks buried their dead within their homes.

The word "cemetery" derives from the Greek and Roman words for "sleeping chamber", according to the Australian Museum, which suggests that although cremation was used by the Romans, it fell out of favour in western Europe for many centuries, partly because those of the Christian faith felt that setting fire to a body might interfere with chances of an afterlife.

Taboos about death continue to restrict speech (and actions) all around the world. In a six-part series on Chinese attitudes to death, the online magazine Sixth Tone revealed how, in China, people will pay extra not to have the number "4" in their mobile telephone number because the word sounds like the Mandarin word for "death".

It also explores why Chinese families don't talk about death and funerals, or even write wills.

In Britain, research by the charity Macmillan Cancer Support found just over a third of the people they surveyed had thoughts or feelings about death that they hadn't shared with anyone. Fears about death concerned 84% of respondents, and one in seven people surveyed opted out of answering the questions about death. →

EDITOR
Rachael Jolley
DEPUTY EDITORS
Jemimah Steinfeld/Sally Gimson
SUB EDITORS
Tracey Bagshaw,
Alex Dudok de Wit

CONTRIBUTING EDITORS
Irene Caselli (Argentina),
Jan Fox (USA),
Kaya Genç (Turkey),
Laura Silvia Battaglia (Yemen and Iraq),
Stephen Woodman (Mexico)

EDITORIAL ASSISTANT
Lewis Jennings
ART DIRECTOR
Matthew Hasteley
COVER
Ben Jennings

THANKS TO
Jodie Ginsberg,
Sean Gallagher,
Ryan McChrystal,
Julia Sherwood
MAGAZINE PRINTED BY
Page Bros.,
Norwich UK

INDEX ON CENSORSHIP
indexcensorship.org | +44 (0) 20 7963 7262 | 292 Vauxhall Bridge Road, London SW1V 1AE, United Kingdom

Supported by
ARTS COUNCIL ENGLAND

These taboos, especially around death and illness, can stop people asking for help or finding support in times of crisis.

Mental health campaigner Alastair Campbell wrote in our winter 2015 issue that when he was growing up, no one ever spoke about cancer or admitted to having it.

It felt like it would bring shame to any family that admitted having it, he remembered. Campbell said that he felt times had moved on and that in Britain, where he lives, there was more openness about cancer these days, although people still struggle to talk about mental health.

Hospice director Elise Hoadley tells one of our writers, Tracey Bagshaw, for her article on the rise of death cafes (p14), that British people used to be better at talking about death because they saw it up close and personal. For instance, during the Victorian period it would be far more typical to have an open coffin in a home, where family or friends could visit the dead person before a funeral. And vicar Laura Baker says of 2018: "When someone dies we are all at sea. We don't know what to do."

In a powerful piece for this issue (p8), Moscow-based journalist Daria Litvinova reports on a campaigning movement in Russia to expose obstetric abuse, with hundreds of women's stories being published. One obstacle to get these stories out is that Russian women are not expected to talk about the troubles they encounter during childbirth. As one interviewee tells Litvinova: "And generally, giving birth, just like anything else related to women's physiology, is a taboo subject." Russian maternity hospitals remain institutions where women often feel isolated, and some do not even allow relatives to visit. "We either talk about the beauty of a woman's body or don't talk about it at all," said one Russian.

Elsewhere, Asian-American women talk to US editor Jan Fox (p27) about why they are afraid to speak to their parents and families about anything to do with sex; how they don't admit to having partners; and how they worry that the climate of fear will get worse with new legislation being introduced in the USA.

As we go to press, not only are there moves to introduce a "gag rule" – which would mean removing funding from clinics that either discuss or offer abortion – but in the state of Ohio, lawmakers are discussing House Bill 565, which would make abortions illegal even if pregnancies arise from rape or incest or which risk the life of the mother. These new laws are likely to make women more worried than before about talking to professionals about abortion or contraception.

Don't miss our special investigation from Honduras, where the bodies of young people are being discovered on a regular basis but their killers are not being convicted. Index's 2018 journalism fellow Wendy Funes reports on p24.

We also look at the taboos around birth and marriage in other parts of the world. Wana Udobang reports from Nigeria (p45), where obstetrician Abosede Lewu tells her how the stigma around Caesarean births still exists in Nigeria, and how some women try to pretend they don't happen — even if they have had the operation themselves. "In our environment, having a C-section is still seen as a form of weakness due to the combination of religion and culture."

CREDIT: iMrSquid/iStock

Meanwhile, there's a fascinating piece from China about how its new two-child policy means women are being pressurised to have more children, even if they don't want them — a great irony when, only a decade ago, if women had a second child they had to pay.

IN OTHER MATTERS, I have just returned from the annual Eurozine conference of cultural journals, this year held in Vienna. It was interesting to hear about a study into the role of this specific type of publication. Research carried out by Stefan Baack, Tamara Witschge and Tamilla Ziyatdinova at the University of Groningen, in the Netherlands, is looking at what long-form cultural journalism does and what it achieves.

The research is continuing, but the first part of the research has shown that this style of magazine or journal stimulates creative communities of artists and authors, as well as creating debates and exchanges across different fields of knowledge. Witschge, presenting the research to the assembled editors, said these publications (often published quarterly) have developed a special niche that exists between the news media and academic publishing, allowing them to cover issues in more depth than other media, with elements of reflection.

She added that in some countries cultural journals were also compensating for the "shortcomings and limitations of other media genres". Ziyatdinova also spoke of the myth of the "short attention span".

At a time when editors and analysts continue to debate the future of periodicals in various forms, this study was heartening. It suggests that there still is an audience for what they describe as "cultural journals" such as ours – magazines that are produced on a regular, but not daily basis which aim to analyse as well as report what is going on around the world.

Lionel Barber, the editor of the Financial Times newspaper, spoke of his vision of the media's future at the James Cameron Memorial Lecture at London's City University in November. As well as arguing that algorithms were not going to take over, he said he was convinced that print had a future. He said: "I still believe

… in China, people will pay extra not to have the number '4' in their mobile telephone number

in the value and future of print: the smart, edited snapshot of the news, with intelligent analysis and authoritative commentary."

His belief in magazines as an item that will continue to be in demand, if they offer something different from something readers have already consumed, was made clear: "Magazines, which also count as print – are they going to just disappear? No. Look at The Spectator, look at the sales of Private Eye."

The vibrancy of the magazine world was also clear at this year's British Society of Magazine Editors awards in London, with hundreds of titles represented. Jeremy Leslie, the owner of the wonderful Magculture shop in London (which stocks Index on Censorship) received a special award for his commitment to print. This innovative shop stocks only magazines, not books, and has carved out a niche for itself close to London's City University. Well done to Jeremy. Index was also shortlisted for the specialist editor of the year award, so we are celebrating as well.

We hope you will continue to show your commitment to this particular magazine, in print or in our beautiful digital version, and think of buying gift subscriptions for your friends at this holiday time (check out https://shop.exacteditions.com/index-on-censorship for a digital subscription from anywhere in the world). We appreciate your support this year, and every year, and may you have a happy 2019.

Yours,

Rachael Jolley,
Index on Censorship editor

CONTENTS

VOLUME 47 NUMBER 04 – WINTER 2018

1   **CAN'T SAY; WON'T SAY** RACHAEL JOLLEY

Why we need to talk about death, birth and marriage. Being silenced can be dangerous

BIRTHS, MARRIAGE AND DEATH

What we are afraid to talk about

8   **LABOUR PAINS** DARIA LITVINOVA

Mothers speak out about the abuse they receive while giving birth in Russian hospitals

11   **WHEN TWO IS TOO MANY** KAROLINE KAN

Chinese women are being told to have two babies now, and many are afraid to say no

14   **CHATTING ABOUT DEATH OVER TEA**
TRACEY BAGSHAW

The British are getting more relaxed about talking about dying, and Stephen Woodman reports on Mexico's Day of the Dead being used for protest

18   **STRIPSEARCH** MARTIN ROWSON

Taboos in the boozer. Death finds a gloomy bunch of stiffs in an English pub...

21   **"DON'T TALK ABOUT SEX"** IRENE CASELLI

Women and girls in Latin America are being told that toothpaste can be used as a contraceptive and other lies about sex

24   **DEATH GOES UNCHALLENGED** WENDY FUNES

Thousands of people are murdered in Honduras every year and no one is talking about it – a special investigation by Index's 2018 journalism fellow

27   **REPRODUCING SILENCE** JAN FOX

Asian-American communities in the USA don't discuss sex, and planned US laws will make talking about abortion and contraception more difficult

31   **A MATTER OF STRIFE AND DEATH** KAYA GENÇ

Funeral processions in Turkey have become political gatherings where "martyrs" are celebrated and mass protests take place. Why?

34   **REST IN PEACE AND ART** LEWIS JENNINGS

Ghanaians are putting the fun into funerals by getting buried in artsy coffins shaped like animals and even Coke bottles

36   **WHEN YOUR BODY BELONGS TO THE STATE** JIEUN BAEK

Girls in North Korea are told that a man's touch can get them pregnant while those who ask about sex are considered a moral and political threat to society

39   **MATERNAL FILM SPARKS ROW** STEVEN BOROWIEC

South Korean men are getting very angry indeed about the planned film adaption of a novel about motherhood

42   **TAKING PRIDE IN CHANGE** JOAN MCFADDEN

Attitudes to gay marriage in Scotland's remote islands are changing slowly, but the strict Presbyterian churches came out to demonstrate against the first Pride march in the Hebrides

45   **SILENCE ABOUT C-SECTIONS** WANA UDOBANG

Nigeria has some of the highest infant and maternal mortality rates in the world, in part, because of taboos over Caesarean sections

48   **WE NEED TO TALK ABOUT GENOCIDE**
ABIGAIL FRYMANN ROUCH

Rwanda, Cambodia and Germany have all dealt with past genocides differently, but the healthiest nations are those which discuss it openly

51 OPPOSITES ATTRACT...TROUBLE
BHEKISISA MNCUBE

Seventy years after interracial marriages were prohibited in South Africa, the author writes about what happened when he married a white woman

....

54 MY YEAR IN REVIEW: SNOWFLAKES AND DIAMONDS JODIE GINSBERG

Under-18s are happy to stand up for free speech and talk to those with whom they disagree

IN FOCUS

58 KILLING THE NEWS RYAN MCCHRYSTAL

Photographer Paul Conroy, who worked with Sunday Times correspondent Marie Colvin, says editors struggle to cover war zones now

61 AN UNDELIVERED LOVE LETTER JEMIMAH STEINFELD

Kite Runner star Khalid Abdalla talks about how his film In the Last Days of the City can't be screened in the city where it is set, Cairo

64 CHARACTER (F)LAWS ALISON FLOOD

Francine Prose, Melvin Burgess, Peter Carey and Mark Haddon reflect on whether they could publish their acclaimed books today

68 MAKE ART NOT WAR LAURA SILVIA BATTAGLIA

Yemeni artists are painting the streets of bombed out cities with their protests

71 TRUTH OR DARE SALLY GIMSON

An interview with Nobel prize-winning author Svetlana Alexievich about her work and how she copes with threats against her

73 FROM ARMED REBELLION TO RADICAL RADIO STEPHEN WOODMAN

Nearly 25 years after they seized power in Chiapas, Mexico, Zapatistas are running village schools and radio stations, and even putting people up for election

CULTURE

78 DANGEROUS CHOICES LIWAA YAZJI

The Syrian writer's new short play about the horror of a mother waiting at home to be killed and then taking matters into her own hands, published for the first time

88 SWEAT THE SMALL STUFF NEEMA KOMBA

Cakes, marriage and how one bride breaks with tradition, a new short story by a young Tanzanian flash fiction writer

94 POWER PLAY YURI HERRERA

This short story by one of Mexico's most famous contemporary authors is about the irrational exercise of power which shuts down others. Translated into English for the first time

....

98 INDEX AROUND THE WORLD: ARTISTS FIGHT ON AGAINST CENSORS LEWIS JENNINGS

Index has run a workshop on censorship of Noël Coward plays and battled the British government to give visas to our Cuban Index fellows 2018 (it took seven months)

....

102 END NOTE: THE NEW "CIVIL SERVICE" TROLLS WHO AIM TO DISTRACT JEMIMAH STEINFELD

The government in China is using its civil servants to act as internet trolls. It's a hard management task generating 450 million social media posts a year

ABOVE: A boy with his face painted at a festival on the outskirts of Morelia, Mexico, just before celebrating the Day of the Dead

SPECIAL
REPORT

☰ BIRTH, MARRIAGEAND DEATH:
  What we are afraid to talk about

08 **LABOUR PAINS** DARIA LITVINOVA

11 **WHEN TWO IS TOO MANY** KAROLINE KAN

14 **CHATTING ABOUT DEATH OVER TEA**
    TRACEY BAGSHAW

18 **STRIPSEARCH** MARTIN ROWSON

21 **"DON'T TALK ABOUT SEX"** IRENE CASELLI

24 **DEATH GOES UNCHALLENGED** WENDY FUNES

27 **REPRODUCING SILENCE** JAN FOX

31 **A MATTER OF STRIFE AND DEATH** KAYA GENÇ

34 **REST IN PEACE AND ART** LEWIS JENNINGS

36 **WHEN YOUR BODY BELONGS TO THE STATE**
    JIEUN BAEK

39 **MATERNAL FILM SPARKS ROW**
    STEVEN BOROWIEC

42 **TAKING PRIDE IN CHANGE** JOAN MCFADDEN

45 **SILENCE ABOUT C-SECTIONS** WANA UDOBANG

48 **WE NEED TO TALK ABOUT GENOCIDE**
    ABIGAIL FRYMANN ROUCH

51 **OPPOSITES ATTRACT... TROUBLE**
    BHEKISISA MNCUBE

Labour pains

Mothers who give birth in Russian hospitals are often yelled at by nurses and left bleeding and shaking. **Daria Litvinova** reports on the women speaking out against obstetric abuse

47(04): 8/10 I DOI: 10.1177/0306422018819304

WHEN ZLATA IVANOVA, pregnant with her son, was admitted to a maternity hospital in her home town of Novosibirsk, Siberia four years ago, she had no idea she would end up struggling with postpartum depression and panic attacks for years afterwards. Her experience was traumatising. She went through several painful pelvic examinations that made her bleed; an on-call doctor told her off for arriving too early; and she had to crawl on all fours to the foetal monitoring procedure room two floors up while having painful contractions without anyone helping her.

Her contractions lasted for 16 hours, and she spent them squirming on a bed covered with a rubber sheet, in pain, not being allowed to get up, and with seven other women writhing in agony in the same room while nurses yelled at them. Without her consent, doctors put her on an oxytocin drip and broke her waters to speed up the process.

When she was finally giving birth, they yelled at her that she was killing her baby. The baby was fine, but they took him away anyway. Three interns stitched up a tear in her vagina without any anaesthetic and left Ivanova, bleeding and shaking, on a gurney in a hospital corridor.

"Aftershocks of it still haunt me," Ivanova, 28, told Index. "I blame myself for not being able to protect myself when giving birth, not [being] prepared for what happened, not considering myself important enough to argue with the medics."

What happened to her is hardly an isolated case, there are hundreds of stories similar to Ivanova's published in #насилие_в_родах

(#violence_in_obstetrics), a community on VK, Russia's biggest social network, that two doulas started in 2016 to raise awareness about obstetric abuse in Russia.

Doulas are professionals trained in childbirth who provide emotional, physical and educational support to pregnant women and new mothers. Many also significantly speak up for and advocate women's wishes during childbirth.

Having worked in this field for years, Maria Ushankova and Yulia Goryachyova have witnessed the abuse firsthand. In 2016, inspired by the #IAmNotAfraidToSpeak campaign on social media, when thousands of women in Russia and Ukraine shared stories about sexual abuse, they decided there was a need for a similar campaign dedicated to obstetric abuse. They came up with a hashtag and called on women to speak up.

The stories poured in almost immediately. "For about two months, we were flooded with stories, receiving 60 or 70 of them a day," Ushankova recalled.

Ivanova posted her story in the community in December 2016, more than two years after she gave birth. She immediately felt better, saying: "Before that, I only talked about it to a couple of people, and not in detail. I feared being judged or, even worse, pitied."

In the two years since then, Ushankova and Goryachova have received and posted more than 850 stories, most of them anonymously. Currently, the VK community has more than 12,000 followers and it provides a rare platform for women to voice their grievances. Very few, if any, women resort to official complaints to hospital administrators or law enforcement. According to Ushankova, women know it is really hard to prove wrongdoing, especially if there are no physical injuries, because doctors and hospital administrators usually protect their own.

"Plus, the mother and the family use all their energy and resources on caring for the newborn baby," she added. "This is why there is no large-scale, mass pushback against obstetric abuse, women just don't have the [emotional and structural] resources to fight." Ushankova

OPPOSITE: Patients in a Moscow maternity ward. Often there are only three to four midwives and four doctors for 30 to 40 women

says the most common issues women complain about are rudeness and humiliating comments from medical staff, their requests being ignored and, most importantly, pain.

"When a woman says that she's in a pain, the response is usually: 'It can't be painful, come on, how are you planning on delivering the baby if you're already in pain?'," she said.

Women are often not allowed to move freely during labour or when they're having contractions, and are forced to lie down.

Then there are procedures like inducing labour, breaking the waters or episiotomy (an incision on the posterior vaginal wall to enlarge the opening for the baby to pass through) that doctors and obstetricians carry out without asking for consent or even warning women about what is going happen.

In a survey Russia's Association of

Without her consent, doctors put her on an oxytocin drip and broke her waters to speed up the process

Professional Doulas conducted last year, polling more than 2,800 mothers from across Russia, 77% of women reported undergoing various procedures when giving birth.

"The vast majority of them told us they were not informed in any way about these procedures," Lyubov Shraibman, a doula from Novosibirsk who worked on the study, told Index.

Obstetricians, midwives and doulas disagree on how serious and widespread the problem is. Some deny it and say it died →

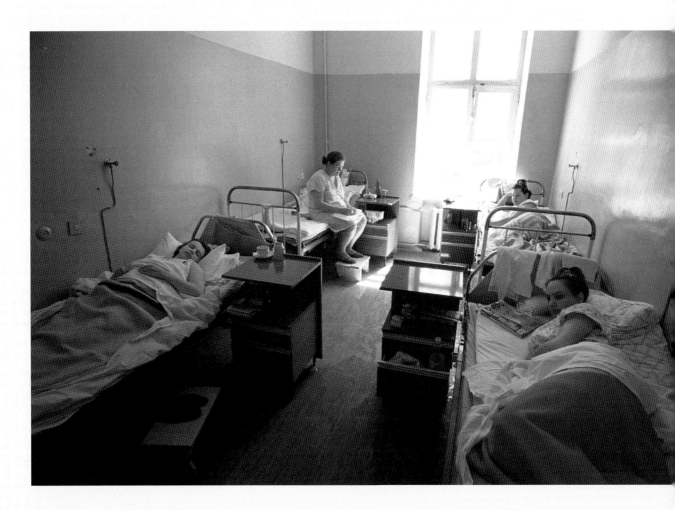

When a woman says that she's in a pain, the response is usually: 'It can't be painful, come on, how are you planning on delivering the baby if you're already in pain?'

→ with the Soviet Union; others insist it's more or less pandemic in maternity hospitals, the vast majority of which are state-run, often understaffed and underfunded.

Everyone agrees, however, that the way the system works today doesn't allow a lot of room for individualised care and for women having a voice.

Many maternity hospitals offer paid-for services that include single rooms and personal midwives, but most women opt for whatever is covered by the state insurance, and that means sharing attention from the doctors with dozens of other women.

"Imagine, it's three to four midwives and four doctors for 30 to 40 women in labour," said Yulia Vuchenovich, an obstetrician and gynaecologist at the state-run Maternity Hospital No. 29 in Moscow.

Working in these conditions, obstetricians and midwives often choose to do what is faster, be it inducing labour or going for a C-section, adds Tatyana Sadovaya, midwife and founder of the Centre for Traditional Midwifery.

"Doctors barely have the time to change their gloves, let alone be nice to women," she said. "They see a medical problem that needs to be solved, not a woman with needs."

Exhausting 24-hour shifts that make doctors and midwifes burn out quickly, and professional habits based on old, procedure-heavy protocols, only add insult to injury.

At the same time, specialists interviewed by Index all agree that the situation has started to change for the better. More and more maternity hospitals offer options that were not available five years ago – such as giving birth with your partner, having a personal obstetrician or doula, a water birth, or giving birth in any position that is more comfortable for a woman, said Lyubov Yerofeyeva, gynaecologist and head of the Moscow-based Population and Development NGO.

Professional standards have improved, too, adds Vuchenovich. A lot of medical procedures that used to be routine and were carried out on all women are now deemed unnecessary, unless there are medical issues that require intervention.

For now, though, Ushankova continues to receive and publish stories of women who are traumatised by what happened in maternity hospitals, and the VK community seems to be the only place for them to talk about it.

"There is very little support for women [who went through obstetric abuse] when it comes to their friends and family," said doula Shraibman. "If a mother is healthy and her baby is healthy, but she continues to cry herself to sleep recalling what happened to her during labour, the reaction usually is: 'Forget it, it's all good, the baby's healthy, time to pull it together'."

Society judges women for having troubles while giving birth, added Ushankova. "Examining a baby, a paediatrician would always ask how the labour went. And if you tell them you had a C-section or induced contractions, they would often say something like: 'Oh really? So you failed to do it on your own, huh?'. It knocks the wind out of a woman."

And, generally, giving birth, just like anything else related to women's physiology, is a taboo subject.

"We either talk about the beauty of a woman's body or don't talk about it at all... Plus, maternity hospitals remain quite closed-up institutions, where even relatives are not always allowed," Ushankova said.

"So the way it works is we send a woman to the hospital, and in a few days she comes out with a pretty little bundle and a smile on her face. What happened in between doesn't really interest anyone." ⊗

Daria Litvinova *is a Moscow-based journalist who focuses on human rights issues*

When two is too many

The Chinese government is now telling women they should have two children but, as **Karoline Kan** finds, many are afraid to say no

47(04): 11/13 I DOI: 10.1177/0306422018819306

WHEN I WENT to my home town for the mid-autumn festival, a Chinese national holiday, I heard my closest cousin, Chunting, the mother of a young boy, had just had an abortion.

"One child is already exhausting me," she said. "You have no idea how expensive it is to raise a child these days. Another one? No way!"

Her mother-in-law was not happy. "While the government now allows a second child, I don't understand why you don't accept it with great joy," she said. "Women of my generation were never given that choice."

After lunch, my cousin and I had a walk in the small town where we grew up. Three years since China announced the replacement of the one-child policy with a two-child policy, I couldn't see any sign of the old slogans that used to be painted on the walls of people's homes or the red banners that hung in business areas, saying either "giving birth to fewer and healthy children makes a happy life" or "[the government] advocates marrying late and having children late". Instead, colourful posters with baby images and slogans such as "[welcome] a new era of [the] two-child policy" are now on bulletin boards in front of local government buildings.

Relaxation of birth control should be a good thing, but not in this way. The Chinese government has not loosened the policy to give women autonomy over their own reproductive rights. Instead its change of policy is the result of demographic fears about an ageing society. For years, double-digit GDP growth has helped the ruling Chinese Communist Party to maintain its political legitimacy. The government is now worried that a shrinking labour force could make the already slowing economy even more gloomy, and the demographic crisis has become one of the party's biggest concerns.

There are many signs that China is launching a new campaign to persuade women to have two children. In August, a subway in Changsha, Hunan province, controversially posted a pink advertisement that read "1001 reasons to have babies" throughout the train carriages. State media newspaper People's Daily published an op-ed recently arguing that "to have babies is not only the business of a family, but also of the country". In some provinces, the local government has tightened the requirements for couples to be able to divorce to keep alive the possibility of new offspring.

Rumours are spreading, too. Stories on social media such as "more restriction on buying condoms and oral contraceptive pills" or "hospitals refuse to carry out abortions" have gone viral. Most of these have proven false or inaccurate. But in a country where the decision-making process is far removed from the average woman's life, rumours related to birth control run rampant. People, including my cousin, worry that such bizarre stories could one day become true, not least given the recent past.

Chinese women are always told to do what we "should do" rather than what we want to do. Women's voices are never respected, whether it's my grandmother's generation or mine. Shortly after the Communist Party took power (in 1949), my grandmother was told by the government that mothers with many →

Women's voices are never respected, whether it's my grandmother's generation or mine

Terms such as 'leftover women' have emerged, levelled at women over the age of 27 who remain single, and women who seek gender equality are called names such as 'feminist bitch'

→ children were "heroine mothers" because Mao wanted the country to be prepared for any potential wars. My grandmother had nine children (two later died). Then my mother's generation was told that China's development couldn't be sustained with an explosive population. The national goal was to "improve the quality of the population" and the one-child policy was the answer. My mother and her friends had no privacy: the local officials ordered all women with one child to be fitted with a contraceptive ring and they were checked regularly in hospital to see that they were still in place. If they broke the rule and had an "illegal child" the government would send them to be sterilised.

I grew up with horrifying stories: women in late-month pregnancy who were forced to have abortions; female infants who were killed or abandoned due to a traditional preference for boys. Both my cousin and I were illegal second children and we saw how the officials chased our parents for fines for "breaking the rule".

And now, women of my generation, born during the one-child policy, are expected to have more children because our country is facing a demographic crisis.

A real feminist movement could be one way for Chinese women to speak out. However, the Chinese government has clamped down on the movement, harassing and arresting prominent feminists.

The pressure to get married and have babies also comes from family and society. Traditional culture regarding gender roles remains strong. Women are expected to take care of family and children. Terms such as "leftover women" have emerged, levelled at women over the age of 27 who remain single, and women who seek

gender equality are called names such as "feminist bitch". These terms shame and silence women.

Like my cousin's mother-in-law, many older Chinese people still believe in the traditional value of "more children, more happiness and luck". In the small northern town where I come from, girls marry as soon as they finish school and get pregnant shortly after. Any exception would be gossiped about. Since the two-child policy began, the pressure has increased. I am turning 30 next year. The number scares my parents. I have no marriage plans and children are not on any to-do list. The topics of marriage and children have become the source of many fights between myself and my parents. I feel that to remain single and childless is committing a crime in the eyes of some.

Right now, the two-child policy hasn't stopped plummeting birthrates. According to the National Bureau of Statistics, 630,000 fewer people were born in 2017 than in 2016. A recent survey done by the All-China Women's Federation shows that only 20.5% of married couples with a child are willing to have a second. Although the two-child policy has not yet increased China's birth rate, it has caused other, negative, results. China Daily said the two-child policy was making it more difficult for women to find jobs. Women have long been discriminated against in the job market. In a survey conducted in 2014 by the Women's Studies Institute of China (WSIC), 86.18% of female graduates in Beijing, Hebei and Shandong have experienced gender discrimination in finding jobs. Employers don't hesitate to ask

RIGHT: A pregnant woman poses in a swimming pool in Shanghai, China in 2014

CREDIT: Carlos Barria/Reuters

female job seekers about their plans for marriage and maternity leave. With the two-child policy, employers prefer male employees, worrying women with one child will take maternity leave again soon for another.

Disadvantage in the job market could weaken women's voices further, especially within marriage. A recent study published in Chinese Sociological Review shows women with less marital power are likelier to succumb to pressure to have a second child even if they do not want to. The findings also show that motherhood is a major contributor to the gender pay gap.

In my cousin Chunting's case, her husband agrees with her decision not to have another child. It's a relief for now. But what if one day he changes his mind? How could she speak up and resist? She depends on him financially. If that happens, she will either have to accept it or face an unpleasant marriage, neither of which are the positive, empowering outcomes she wants to see. ⊗

Karoline Kan *is a Beijing-based writer and journalist*

Chatting about death over tea

Death cafes are popping up across the UK.
Tracey Bagshaw speaks to an organiser of one
and asks whether the British reluctance to talk
about the end of life is eroding

47(04): 14/17 I DOI: 10.1177/0306422018819307

EVERY MONTH, ALL around the UK, groups
of people get together to talk about something most of us try not to contemplate – death.
In many cases, we British won't even say the
word. We have a wide collection of euphe-
misms, ranging from the comedic – kicked the
bucket, popped his clogs – to the whimsical
– passed away, gone to sleep or even lost, like
an umbrella which might turn up unexpectedly.
But people who visit death cafes are more than
happy to talk about it.

The cafes are based on the work of anthropologist Bernard Crettaz, who held the
first *café mortel* in Switzerland in 2004. His
aim was to break the "tyrannical secrecy"
surrounding the topic of death; the idea soon
caught on around the world.

The first in the UK was held in 2011, and Su
Squire facilitates the one in Norwich.

More pop-up events than permanent cafes,
they attract people from all walks of life for tea
and cake (an important aspect of the more than
7,000 cafes worldwide), and aim "to increase
awareness of death with a view to helping
people make the most of their (finite) lives".

"We talk about everything that comes up,"
said Squire. "People talk about funerals, whether there's an afterlife, what a good death would
be, living wills, the right to die, legacies … They
are actually very life-affirming events.

"It's all about connection. The only thing we
all share is death."

The Co-op, a leading funeral provider in the
UK, has just completed the first national
survey of its kind into attitudes towards
death, with over 30,000 people taking part.
Managing director Robert Maclachlan says
he hopes the survey will show that "there is
a huge opportunity to reduce the emotional
and financial burden that occurs following
a death, simply by people opening up more
about these issues".

According to the research, the average age
when people in the UK experience the loss of
someone close to them for the first time is 20.
A quarter (24%) first experience it by the age
of 10, but only 16% have been to a funeral
at that age, which suggests that many young-
sters are kept away from death. And yet
research carried out at the University of East
Anglia shows that children are keen to discuss
death from a very young age. They are fascinated
by dead animals they come across and are
inquisitive, but parents often bat their questions
away, making death scarier than it needs to be.

And so we try not to think about it.

Only around a quarter of us (27%) have
made wills, a mere 5% have funeral plans and
just 19% have put something aside to pay for
our funerals, making for potential financial
trouble ahead.

Aside from funerals, there are few rituals
around death in traditional British culture. But
there is bureaucracy to cope with and funerals
have to be arranged – usually with no real idea
of what to do.

Sarah Jones started Full Circle Funerals two
years ago. She encourages people to talk about
their funerals well in advance.

"Somehow we think that if we talk about
death, it will make it more likely, or we don't
like talking about it because we don't want to
upset the person we are talking to," she said.
"It's also a coping strategy to deny its existence.

*When you allow yourself to
accept that death is part of
life, it's incredibly liberating*

CREDIT: Marco Jeurissen

MARCOJEURISSEN.NL

But talking about death, as well as planning for it, can give peace of mind."

When she is out socially, people love to ask her questions about death: how is the body prepared? What happens to it? She says that while many agree that talking would be a good thing, we haven't quite got there yet.

"It's a downwards spiral," she said. "We don't talk about it because we can't deal with it and because we don't know how to deal with it, we don't talk about it …"

But we surround ourselves with death all the time. Some of the bestselling books over the past few years have been about terminal illness – The Fault in Our Stars, Me Before You and Before I Die, for example. Crime novels fly off the shelves and music takes death in all its forms as a common subject.

Some patients hold it all together, being strong because they don't want to be a burden or upset their family, then fall apart when they have gone

→ Clothing featuring skulls entwined with roses or snakes is mainstream, and tattooists report a rise in people asking for designs featuring memento mori (a symbol to remind us that death is always nearby). Our fashion choices are bringing our mortality to the fore, albeit unwittingly, as tattooist Gee from Norwich studio Enter the Void explains.

"We don't have people who come in and ask for things about death," he said. "On the whole it's less morbid and more about the artwork. Skulls are beautiful things."

So if we are happy to be surrounded by images of death, why are we still so reluctant to talk about it?

Earlier this year, the charity Sue Ryder started the #FacingLossTogether campaign, calling for an open conversation about death after a study revealed how little most people knew about it – and how much it worried them. The campaign is in its early days; hospice director Elise Hoadley says it is presenting opportunities to broach the subject, including on social media, and hopes that more people will open up as a result. She says death never used to be such a taboo subject.

"As a nation, we don't talk about death like we used to. The Victorians were very into death. Now we are more clinical because death isn't around us so much. Babies died, mothers died in childbirth, people lived in family units and watched people die in the same house, so they were more used to it."

Our love of death as entertainment has probably not helped.

"Death on TV is all about murders, war, terrorism, violence," she added. "Most death is not like that."

Working in hospices, Hoadley sees both the dying and their families. She says they all react

differently, but the stiff-upper-lip approach is often applied on both sides.

"Some patients hold it all together, being strong because they don't want to be a burden or upset their family, then fall apart when they have gone. Some families don't want to talk about it because they don't want to upset the person who is dying."

Today's Britain is made up of people of many cultures and faiths, but there is still a common thread around death. David Collingwood, director of funerals for Co-op Funeralcare, told Index that Hindus are the most uncomfortable talking about their own death, with 51% saying this is the case. And, despite being encouraged by Islam to accept death and make plans, one in five Muslims is frightened of it. Jews were shown to be the most comfortable, with a quarter saying they considered their own mortality when they were less than 10 years old. Maybe for that reason, one in five (18%) has a funeral plan in place.

Death is an everyday topic for Laura Baker.

DAY OF THE PROTESTING DEAD

| | | | | | | | | | | | | | | | | | | | | | | | | | | | | | | | | | | | | | | | | | | | | |

Mexico's celebration of deceased ancestors is a great way to talk about death – and injustice, writes STEPHEN WOODMAN

WITH SKELETON PARADES, sugar skulls and candlelit altars, Mexico's Day of the Dead is a feast for the senses. But the annual celebration – which runs from 31 October to 2 November – also serves a freedom of expression purpose. As well as challenging taboos around death, the festival has become an occasion for protest in Mexico.

While historians say the celebration has Mesoamerican origins, many of its modern elements developed in the late 19th century. With Mexico in the grip of a repressive dictatorship, newspapers would publish poems, known as *calaveras*, to mark the festivities. These mock eulogies offered a rare opportunity to poke fun at politicians and the clergy. The poems were often printed alongside cartoons depicting public figures as skeletons.

José Guadalupe Posada was a noted *calavera*

CREDIT: iStock by Getty Images

In her work as a Church of England vicar she talks to parishioners who are dying, worried relatives and people arranging funerals.

"When someone dies, we are all at sea," she said. "We don't know what to do. Most of us never see a dead body – I haven't seen a dead body – but that's normal. Most people are 40 before they see one. For the first time in history we are so detached from death.

"I would say I am still scared of it, but it has got a lot easier for me to talk about it. I'm 29 and I have made a will and decided whether I want to be buried or cremated."

Belief in the afterlife can be a comfort, Baker says. And even those who say they are not religious lean on its imagery.

"They say someone is looking down on them, or that they are smiling down and protecting them, or they are with someone else who has died," she said. "Saying things like that give some comfort that their loved ones are not alone."

Still, as Squire of the Norwich cafe says,

we see it as something to be beaten rather than embraced.

"Advances in science mean we can live longer and people are brought back from the brink of death. It's become a challenge, something we fight against," she said. "When you allow yourself to accept that death is part of life, it's incredibly liberating." ⊗

Tracey Bagshaw is a freelance journalist and editor, based in Norwich, UK

printmaker. His most famous creation, La Catrina, has become an iconic Day of the Dead image. The cartoon depicts a skeleton in a European-style dress – a satirical stab at the Mexican elite.

"The vantage point is death as a leveller," said Claudio Lomnitz, the author of Death and the Idea of Mexico. "The contrast is always between the quality of the bones and the pretension of the dress."

The Day of the Dead reflects Mexico's unique openness to the topic of death. Mexican literary icons such as the novelist Juan Rulfo and the poet Octavio Paz deal with the theme extensively in their work, while newspapers still splash highly graphic photos of crime scenes across their front pages. The celebration also encourages people to think about their own mortality. Food and altars for the deceased bring representations of death into the home.

The festival has taken on a political dimension, too, as death and bereavement have become central issues. In 2006, the government deployed troops to fight the country's drug cartels, triggering violence that has left more than 215,000 dead. Low conviction rates fuel this cycle of bloodshed. According to the 2017 Global Impunity Index published by Mexico's Universidad de Las Américas, the country has the highest rate of impunity on the American continent. Against that backdrop, protesters use the festival to draw attention to the victims of the bloodshed.

For last year's Day of the Dead, campaigners marched in Mexico City to commemorate women murdered in the country. The previous year, protesters placed an altar at a train station in the capital to honour the murdered transgender activist Alessa Flores.

"The radical root [of the festival] runs very deep," Lomnitz said. "I do believe there's a recovery of that tradition... The Days of the Dead have become a space for protest."

Stephen Woodman is a contributing editor (Mexico) at Index on Censorship

ABOVE: Women in Mexico dressed as La Catrina during the Day of the Dead festival

Rowson

47(04): 18/19 | DOI: 10.1177/0306422018819308

MARTIN ROWSON
is a cartoonist for
The Guardian and
the author of various
books, including
The Communist
Manifesto (2018), a
graphic novel adap-
tion of the famous
19th century book

Metal presents

VILL AGE GRE EN.

SAT 13 JULY 2019
11AM-9PM
CHALKWELL PARK, SOUTHEND ON SEA

45 MINUTES FROM LONDON

ESSEX BEST LOVED ARTS FESTIVAL
TICKETS ON SALE - 20 NOV
VILLAGEGREENFESTIVAL.COM

CHRISTMAS PROMO
20% DISCOUNT - ENDS 24 DEC

PHOTO : TIGGS DA AUTHOR, VG16 BY CLARISSA DEBENHAM

10

"Don't talk about sex"

Women across Latin America speak to **Irene Caselli** about contraception, legalising abortion and Brazil's new president Jair Bolsonaro

47(04): 21/23 | DOI: 10.1177/0306422018819312

AS JAIR BOLSONARO takes over as new president of Brazil on 1 January, women's rights organisations across Latin America and the Caribbean will be holding their breath. A former army captain, Bolsonaro is backed by millions of evangelical Christians who praise his anti-abortion stance. After a campaign marked by misogynist, homophobic and racist comments, women are afraid his conservative stance will take a toll on women's rights in Brazil, negatively influencing the rest of the continent.

"They are classifying women into good and bad, into pure and promiscuous," said Nalu Faria, a psychologist at the Brazil chapter of the World March of Women international feminist movement. "The belief is that those who are on the wrong side, be they black people, working-class people, women or the LGBT community, ought to be punished."

Faria believes that this conservative stance will have an impact, especially on the youngest.

"The little sexual education there is in schools now is going to disappear under the new government," said Faria. "There is a moral

---

The woman said that she thought she had successfully avoided pregnancies by having intercourse when she had a green vaginal discharge – which is, in fact, a sign of infection

---

crusade against the so-called gender ideology, and sexual education is going to fall victim of this."

But Brazil is not an isolated case in Latin America when it comes to women's reproductive rights being endangered by ultra-conservatives.

When Daniela López's parents found a condom in her room in Mexico City, all hell broke loose.

"There was no dialogue, no questions asked. They scolded me and said that no condoms were allowed in the house," López said.

She was 16 at the time, and was not sexually active. She had received the condom at a health centre without any explanation. There were no sex education classes in her school, and the subject was banned at home.

"There is a taboo around contraception, and it starts with the idea of sexuality. Society teaches us girls that we need to preserve ourselves until marriage, so there is no talking about contraception. Even when we get married, contraception is not on the table, because the aim of marriage is conception," said López.

Now 23, she studies teaching methods and gives workshops to adolescents about contraception. She says that most girls are worried about becoming infertile if they use intra-uterine devices or hormonal methods such as the pill. At the same time, they find condoms unreliable because they have to negotiate their use with their partners.

Samady Baldelomar Menacho, an 18-year-old high school student in Bolivia, shares a similar experience.

She is part of a network called Tu Decides (You Decide) and leads sex education workshops in her school in the city of Santa Cruz, where teenage pregnancy rates are the highest in the country.

"When a girl wants to ask a question, she feels ashamed. Only men are free to talk about sex here. If a girl asks a question, they look at her like she is crazy or a bad person," she said. "It is the result of a long chain of machismo. My mum taught me and my grandmother taught my mother: women stay in the

ABOVE: A women's rights activist demonstrating in favour of legalising abortion in Sao Paulo, Brazil

→ kitchen to serve men and obey, while men are in charge. So it is the men who decide if contraception is used or not.

"Because of the taboo around contraception, there has been an epidemic of teenage pregnancies."

In Latin America and the Caribbean, 62% of women aged 15-49 want to avoid a pregnancy. However, 22% of them are not using an effective contraceptive method, according to a 2015 report by the United Nations Population Fund and the Guttmacher Institute.

"Patriarchal traditions and culture continue existing in certain sectors of Latin American society," Esteban Caballero, regional director of UNFPA for Latin America and the Caribbean, told Index. "Patriarchy wants to keep its control over women's fertility."

The ineffective use of contraception takes a staggering toll, especially on the youngest. The latest report by the Pan-American Health Organisation, published in 2018, says that Latin America and the Caribbean is the sole region in the world where under-15 pregnancies are on the

rise, and it is surpassed only by sub-Saharan Africa when it comes to teen pregnancies.

The taboo around contraception also has other serious consequences. In indigenous, remote areas, women are often told what to do to prevent pregnancies by shamans or local midwives who lack medical knowledge and often suggest methods that are dangerous.

In Ecuador's Amazonian region, health workers have reported cases of women who used toothpaste after having sexual intercourse to wash off the sperm. Toothpaste cannot kill sperm, but it can lead to vaginal irritations or infections.

Irlanda Morales, a 24-year-old medical student, is part of a network that promotes reproductive rights in Chiapas, Mexico. She told Index that she was once approached by a woman who believed contraception was immoral. The woman said that she thought she had successfully avoided pregnancies by having intercourse when she had a green vaginal discharge – which is, in fact, a sign of infection.

Unwanted pregnancies may also end in abortions, which are often unsafe in a region where more than 97% of women of reproductive age live under restrictive abortion laws. The US-based Guttmacher Institute calculates that 10% of all maternal deaths in Latin America are due to unsafe abortions.

Legalising abortion has been an uphill battle in many Latin American countries, where the Catholic Church has mobilised against it. Last August, the church backed the Argentinian senators who rejected a bill to legalise abortion.

"I believe that the strong taboos and myths

In Ecuador's Amazonian region, health workers have reported cases of women who used toothpaste after having sexual intercourse to wash off the sperm

related to the use of contraception in Latin America are a result of the teachings of the Catholic church's hierarchy," said María Consuelo Mejía, director of the Mexican chapter of Catholic Women for the Right to Choose, a movement spanning Latin America.

For instance, emergency contraception has been banned in Honduras because of the idea that taking the morning-after pill is tantamount to abortion.

Baldelomar Menacho points out that the lack of information makes it possible for sexual abuse to remain widespread and to go unreported. Data suggests that under-15 pregnancies are often a result of rape or early marriage.

Youth-friendly services can challenge these taboos, she says.

"When we are among peers, there is more trust. Even women feel free to ask more questions. Adults can teach about sexuality and contraception, too, as long as they treat us with respect."

Despite the rise of conservative, religious attitudes, such as Bolsonaro's, over the past years, Latin America has also seen a rise of women-led and youth-led movements. For example, the so-called green wave in favour of legalising abortion in Argentina inspired similar campaigns across the region, with women sharing their stories of illegal abortions and talking freely about sex education. Despite the political predominance of conservatives around the continent, the battle to break down sexual taboos is slowly being won. ⊗

Irene Caselli is contributing editor to Index on Censorship, based in Argentina

Death goes unchallenged

Thousands of killings of young people in Honduras go uninvestigated. In a special report **Wendy Funes** looks at why no one discusses what is happening

47(04): 24/26 | DOI: 10.1177/0306422018819313

AS JUAN ORLANDO Hernández celebrates his fifth year as Honduras president in January, his campaign promise to address high homicide rates in the Central American country seems to have been little more than a slogan.

This autumn the bodies of two young men were discovered just outside Tegucigalpa, the capital. They had their hands tied behind their backs and each one had been shot in the head.

Their crime: to have taken part in anti-government protests. There was no investigation and no one was prosecuted.

Summary executions and murders are part of ordinary life for people in Honduras. No wonder, then, that for this and other reasons an estimated 4,000 Hondurans are fleeing for the US border. And some of these are young people who fear for their lives.

According to Casa Alianza, a foundation that focuses on children's and youth rights, there have been more than 3,000 arbitrary extra-judicial killings of children and youths under the age of 23 since Hernández took over – not a great change from previous years.

Even teenagers at middle schools and primary schools are targets. Sometimes their parents and families are killed if they try to investigate.

Those who kill – criminals and the state – do so with impunity and just 10% face trial. Honduras has one of the highest rates of impunity worldwide, but it has become almost taboo to discuss it.

Anthropologist Bertilio Amaya explains that, faced with the scale of killings from all sides, the population has become used to violence. "Death is perceived as normalised, [as] everyday. People don't get frightened, they don't become indignant," he told Index.

It is a regular occurrence for bodies to turn up on the banks of rivers, with their hands bound and bullet holes in their heads.

Crime scenes read like a map of the country's northern waterways – the Ulúa, the Chamelecón, the Bermejo and the Río Piedras. But the highest number of bodies are found by the River Choluteca in Tegucigalpa.

Nery Ordóñez, former head of criminal investigations for the Honduran national police, revealed in an interview with Index that 1,522 students met with violent deaths between 2010 and 2018. Of these, more than half were young people in middle or secondary school, while 121 were university students.

Ordóñez believes gangs and delinquent groups, and their territorial disputes, rather than police officers or military

> *Even teenagers at middle schools are targets. Sometimes their parents and families are killed if they try to investigate*

personnel are behind the deaths of middle
school students.

Maras, the street gangs that originated
in the USA and now operate across Central
America, are known for their cruelty and
violence. But police investigations do not
usually look for motives behind executions,
and human rights organisations say that these

gangs often kill on behalf of the military and
police. This makes it hard to know who is
doing the killing.

Hernández's government was first elected in
2013 on a promise of reducing the homicide
rate – then 79 per 100,000 inhabitants.

He took office in 2014, and when he was
re-elected for a second term in 2017 the →

BELOW: Protests
sparked by the re-
election of Honduran
President Juan
Orlando Hernandez,
under whose leader-
ship thousands of
deaths have not been
investigated

Death is perceived as normalised, [as] everyday. People don't get frightened, they don't become indignant

→ rate had dropped to 43 per 100,000, according to the Observatory of Violence of the Autonomous University of Honduras.

Hernández was the first Honduran president to run for a second term, after a controversial decision by the country's supreme court to lift a ban on re-election. US support was also instrumental to his success in an election which the opposition claims was rigged.

During protests sparked by the election and allegations of electoral fraud, more than 23 deaths occurred, which a report by the UN High Commission says have been attributed to state security services.

According to the Coalition Against Impunity, a network of 53 human rights NGOs, only one police officer has been charged to date.

The former head of the national police's internal affairs unit, María Luisa Borjas, who was removed from her post after accusing police officers of carrying out summary executions

HONDURAS FACTFILE

||||||||||||||||||||||||||||||||||||||||||||||||||

- President of Honduras Juan Orlando Hernández has been both head of state and head of government since January 2014
- The country gained independence from Spain in 1821
- Two Honduran cities, Distrito Central and San Pedro Sula, rank as two of the top five most violent cities in the world with the latter having 112.09 homicides per 100,000 residents
- Honduras can be a deadly place to work as a reporter. It is the most dangerous country in the Americas for journalists per capita
- The country rates the second poorest in the Central America, with high unemployment and unequal distribution of income

Sources: Global Edge, UCL, The Independent, Al Jazeera, CIA

in 2002, is now a member of congress for the opposition. "There's a policy of killing young people," she claimed.

On two occasions she has spoken up in the National Congress to condemn summary executions. In retaliation, she says, the president no longer gives her the floor.

She told Index of a young man who was abducted at a demonstration when people went on pot-banging protests in defiance of the curfew in December 2017.

The men who attacked him were dressed in civilian clothing but had a military appearance. The young man, who was a leader of protests against the curfew, was abducted one day at 8pm. His body appeared the following day in a street in the Las Hadas district of the capital, bearing signs of torture.

Lawyer Joaquín Mejía, who has also worked at the human rights group Equipo de reflexión, investigación y comunicación and at Radio Progreso, has studied the composition of death squads, gangs and delinquent groups in Honduras.

"Society is well aware that social cleansing squads are operating in Honduras," he said.

One of the groups which became targets of the violence was the Antorchas de Los Indignados (Torches of the Indignant) movement, which was set up in 2015 after a government corruption scandal that included the misappropriation of social security funds.

The most high-profile death was that of lawyer Kevin Ferrera, the legal representative of the leader of Los Indignados. After he was murdered for organising a protest, other high-profile figures went into exile or hiding.

In Mejia's view, execution is a censored topic in Honduras, but the death squads have not gone away.

He says the same groups that played a fundamental role in the 1980s, during the forced disappearances, continue to play a role to this day – invisible and acting with impunity. ⊗

Wendy Funes is a journalist based in Honduras and an Index 2018 journalism fellow

Reproducing silence

As the Trump administration introduces the "gag rule" this winter, conversations about contraception and abortion are going to be even more difficult for Asian-American women, reports **Jan Fox**

47(04): 27/30 I DOI: 10.1177/0306422018819314

"**IN MY EXPERIENCE** sex is very taboo as a topic and there's no expectation of pleasure; it's just tied to marriage and producing children," said Tania Chatterjee, co-founder of the South Asian Sexual and Mental Health Alliance, whose parents emigrated to the USA from India.

"It's heartbreaking that we can't talk about these things in families. There's a very real fear culture around it – of being disowned, of bringing guilt and shame on the family. If we talked to our parents they might surprise us and be OK with it, but we don't know how they will react so we just can't take the risk. They grew up in a different world so I understand, but it doesn't make it any easier," she added.

This often results in living dual lives.

"Because we can't freely express ourselves about sexuality, we present as one person to our community but have 'other lives' with different personalities we show in different situations. Reputation is everything in our culture and how people perceive you and your family is vital, so we can't even share things with the closest friends sometimes."

Winnie Ng, 36, a video editor living in Seattle, was born in Hong Kong and emigrated to New York with her parents as a baby.

"It was definitely taboo to talk about anything to do with sex when I was growing up. My parents just told me: 'You shouldn't date' when I was in high school so I never told them

I had a boyfriend, even in my 20s. I was dating the man who is now my husband for two years before they knew. Luckily I had good sex-ed at school in New York because it was the early '90s and there was a lot of talk about AIDS."

Jaclyn Dean is policy associate for the National Asian Pacific American Women's Forum. The daughter of Taiwanese immigrants, Dean wasn't as lucky on the sex education front.

"I grew up in Texas where the lack of sex-ed in schools didn't help. In ninth grade we were just shown graphic photos of people with STDs [sexually transmitted diseases] like gonorrhea. It was super awkward to talk about sexual health at home, and even now it's not considered mainstream as a health topic when you're growing up Asian-American."

Another Sasmha co-founder, comedian Sriya Sarkar, had a similar experience: "I self-censored when I was young, like never even telling my parents that my friends were dating because I didn't want them thinking I was hanging out with 'wayward' people."

It's the reason Sarkar has not been able to tell her parents to this day that she had an abortion.

"After college I had started doing volunteer work and unexpectedly became pregnant and had an abortion. By then I was old enough to do it on my own insurance so I didn't have to tell anyone," she said.

She decided to turn the experience into a stand-up comedy show. →

My parents know I do a lot around reproductive rights through my work, and I would really love to tell them about my abortion, but there's that perceived fear very much at play

ABOVE: Pro-choice campaigners demonstrate in New York, 2017

CREDIT: Andrew Kelly/Reuters

"I had started doing stand-up about a year before and I just decided to do stuff on abortion. For me it's the way to combat stigma – comedy helps manage things and makes things more accessible and the show, which is poignant as well as funny, has had a really good response, although I'm mostly preaching to the choir. My parents know I do a lot around reproductive rights through my work, and I would really love to tell them about my abortion, but there's that perceived fear very much at play."

The silencing of these conversations has a very negative effect on Asian-American and Pacific Islander women. Dean says they are less likely to use effective contraception: "If you look at AAPI women's contraception usage, it's

lower than that of white women and tends to
be the cheaper, less effective kind. For example,
the pill is effective, but only 57% of AAPI
women have ever used it compared with 89%
of white women … Condoms – used by 24% of
AAPI woman as against 10% of women – are
cheap, but not so effective but they are easier
for AAPI women to access because they don't

have to make an appointment or ask a family
member to make an appointment with a doctor
to get them. The calendar or rhythm method is
also used." How much worse can US President
Donald Trump's administration's proposals
make things?

"Asian-American women are already silenced
on reproductive health by their culture, by →

This 'gag rule' is about silencing doctors and limiting options for women

→ lack of good sex education and sometimes by language barriers, too, which is why Planned Parenthood is so important and why it will be really scary if the Title X domestic 'gag' rule on family planning takes effect," said Dean.

Established in 1970, Title X offers affordable birth control and reproductive health care, mostly to people on low incomes. Earlier this year Trump proposed a nationwide "gag" rule, which would make it illegal for any provider in the Title X programme to discuss abortion or tell patients how to safely and legally access abortion.

"If clinics receiving Title X funding (such as Planned Parenthood, who also use it for access to birth control and STD testing) can't use the money to perform, or refer women for, abortions, what does that look like for someone who needs one? … The crisis health clinics opening up often right next door to Planned Parenthood are funded by conservatives and religious groups and their aim is to talk women out of abortions. If you are an immigrant with limited English and you're already finding it hard to know where to go and what to do, how are you supposed deal with that kind of pressure? This gag rule is about silencing doctors and limiting options for women."

Dean is also very concerned about the Sex and Race Selective Abortion Ban, which is already law in eight states, including Arizona. It requires women to give a reason why they want an abortion and has been criticised for stigmatising Asian-American women through the false stereotype that Asians might choose boys over girls.

"It's asking what is a 'good' and what is a 'bad' reason for an abortion and it criminalises doctors and patients and puts a lot of Asian-American women in an uncomfortable situation. Why would they want to tell someone why they want an abortion? It's a hard enough decision. This kind of fear shouldn't apply to women in this position," said Dean.

There is some hope on the horizon, though. Dean welcomes the recent appointment of the first Asian-American president of Planned Parenthood, Leana Wen. Wen, a Chinese immigrant, showed her fighting spirit in her previous role as health commissioner for Baltimore by suing the Trump administration when they cut Title X funding from a teenage pregnancy prevention programme and won the case. On her appointment to Planned Parenthood she declared on their website:

"Reproductive health care is health care… and healthcare has to be understood as a fundamental human right… We have to do everything that we can to fight."

Chatterjee, who co-founded Sasmha in 2016 to provide a safe space for young south Asian women and men to talk about taboo issues related to sexual and mental health, also has hope.

"We didn't know what to expect when we launched, but we've had a very good response from both women and men looking for a space to talk about these issues that they can't talk about within the family," she said.

"Sasmha helps young south Asian women (and men) to know they are not alone and we need to create more safe spaces like it. I'm also hoping the amount of resilience and passion around politics right now is going to make women braver about having this conversation." ⊗

Jan Fox is contributing editor (USA) for Index on Censorship. She is based in Los Angeles

A matter of strife and death

The arrest of a university student for attending a funeral has unsettled Turkey. As the trial continues, **Kaya Genç** looks at how death has become political in his country

47(04): 31/33 | DOI: 10.1177/0306422018819315

IN DEEPLY POLARISED Turkey death has become an increasingly divisive issue since the 1980s, when the violent clashes between Kurdish militants and the Turkish army began. More recently, the state's attitude towards funeral attendance came to the fore in the case of Berkay Ustabaş. On 5 January 2018, a Turkish Swat team raided the apartment where Ustabaş, a sociology student at Istanbul University, lived with his mother. It was just after 3am when cops took Ustabaş into custody. The prosecutor considered the student's books on Marxist organisations as criminal evidence and asked an Istanbul court to arrest him. As he was taken to a high-security prison, Ustabaş learned that his attendance at a funeral four years previously was among his alleged crimes.

The Turkish state is wary of funeral processions, particularly crowded and politically significant ones. In those ceremonies, the bringing of the casket to the grave can revitalise a century-long animosity between the Turkish state and its longtime opponents: Kurdish nationalists, Marxists and fundamentalists from different Islamic sects. Since plain clothes policemen often patrol the funerals of major political figures, attendees can sometimes find themselves in peril.

In the 1980s, the government and media started to call fallen Turkish soldiers "martyrs" and consider them sacred. The use of "martyred" is now close to mandatory for journalists reporting on the deaths of these soldiers. Militant groups among Marxists and Kurdish nationalists also consider their deceased militants as "martyrs".

As politicised events, funeral processions have come to signify a larger Turkish obsession with death. According to legend, the reflection of the crescent moon and a star in a pool of blood during wartime inspired the design of the Turkish flag; the Turkish national anthem is woven with images of death. These associations help to turn funeral processions into political gatherings.

Although Turkish politicians, from the nationalist Devlet Bahçeli to the Islamist Recep Tayyip Erdogan, occasionally criminalise burial ceremonies, they may also sometimes use them for political propaganda. For those in power, a speech delivered alongside the coffin of a fallen soldier is an effective political tool which they take advantage of. Because funerals serve as spaces for political expression, they become subjected to censorship and even suppression.

Ustabaş was arrested on the birthday of Berkin Elvan, a 15-year-old Turkish boy who died in March 2014, after being hit in the head by a gas canister during anti-government protests. Since his attendance at Elvan's funeral got him into trouble, Ustabaş assumed his arrest on Elvan's birthday was intentional.

The funeral of Elvan, a secondary-school student, was attended by several thousand mourners who chanted anti-government slogans. In response, Turkish police used water cannons and tear gas to disperse the crowd. During the ceremony, a police camera →

Ustabaş learned that his attendance at a funeral four years previously was among his alleged crimes

For those in power, a speech delivered alongside the coffin of a fallen soldier is an effective political tool

→ filmed Ustabaş walking alongside protesters carrying a placard that read: "Elvan's funeral will be avenged."

Ustabaş's arrest is part of a series of controversies involving political funerals. Ragıp Zarakolu, a leading publisher and dissident, lost his wife and co-publisher Ayşe Nur Zarakolu in 2002. At her funeral, the couple's son Deniz Zarakolu, a university student like Ustabaş, delivered a speech about his commitment to his parents' progressive struggle. Soon afterwards, a prosecutor charged him with inciting hatred. In 2011, both Ragıp and Deniz Zarakolu were arrested, alongside approximately 4,000 accused members of the Kurdistan Communities Union (KCK), an illegal organisation demanding Kurdish independence.

Among the most chilling recent political funeral processions was that of Hatun Tuğluk, who died in September 2017. She was the mother of Aysel Tuğluk, a parliamentarian from the pro-Kurdish Peoples' Democratic Party (HDP). Aysel, who is serving a 10-year sentence for terrorism offences, was brought to her mother's funeral on a special permit. But her arrival angered nationalists who claimed that "terrorists" and "martyrs" couldn't be buried in the same cemetery.

Around a dozen protesters initially came to the burial. Using social media, they soon attracted dozens of like-minded anti-Kurdish nationalists. Those who wanted to halt the burial ceremony approached the site driving tractors, vans and cars, and chanting the slogan "this is not an Armenian graveyard" in unison. Nationalist Turks often use the term "Armenian" to denigrate all those deemed to belong to subversive groups.

Tuğluk's relatives were forced to dig up the coffin. Eventually, they brought it to another graveyard and reburied it. When Interior Minister Süleyman Soylu received the news, he rushed to the first burial site, his ministry stated, to make sure "it was safe". In June 2018, Soylu was involved in another row about political funerals when he banned anyone from the main opposition Republican People's Party (CHP), founded by Mustafa Kemal Atatürk in 1919, from the funerals of fallen Turkish soldiers. The government has accused the CHP of supporting Kurdish militants.

Gündüz Vassaf, a Turkish psychologist and the author of Prisoners of Ourselves: Totalitarianism in Everyday Life, considers such events as symptomatic of Turkey's political culture over the last half-century.

"In the 1970s, as a member of a university teachers' union, I attended so many political funerals," Vassaf remembered. "Once I was in the front row of a procession, when a military commander ordered soldiers patrolling the funeral to 'march' toward us. Fearing violence, I caught the eyes of soldiers and ordered back: 'Stop marching!' The soldiers followed both orders in succession, and we were able to lay the coffin to rest."

Vassaf headed Amnesty International's first Turkish branch in Istanbul in the 1970s. He remembers the difficulty of even visiting the graves of Deniz Gezmiş, Yusuf Aslan and Hüseyin İnan, leading members of the illegal People's Liberation Army of Turkey (THKO) who were executed in 1972. The same applied to visiting the graves of right-wing politicians, including Adnan Menderes, Turkey's first democratically elected prime minister, who was executed in 1961 by a military junta. Vassaf says that "people were afraid of being tagged".

Ustabaş, the arrested student, apparently didn't share that fear. "The martyrs of the revolution are immortal," he is accused of shouting during Elvan's funeral. The

prosecutor considered this a call for vengeance. After the funeral procession, an illegal left-wing group attacked a police station; in March 2015, two members of the Revolutionary People's Liberation Party-Front (DHKP-C) took a prosecutor hostage and fatally shot him to "avenge Elvan's death".

Vassaf says that the animosity between the state and its critics continues beyond funeral ceremonies. Aziz Nesin, the great Turkish contrarian and humorist, died in 1995, leaving a will that expressed his wish to be buried in the garden of an educational organisation he founded. But Turkish law forbids burials in private properties; Turkish MPs had to debate the issue in the parliament, and eventually granted Nesin the right to a private burial. But this, they said, was an exception.

"When a Turkish citizen dies, the family is obliged to hand the identity card of the deceased to the state," Vassaf said. When his own mother died some years ago, Vassaf refused to hand back her identity card, as the law required. "I told the authorities that it was lost." Vassaf feels this gesture is symbolically important.

But for those who have years to live ahead of them, like Ustabaş, this is not an option. On the third hearing of his case in September 2018, Ustabaş was not allowed into the courtroom and instead gave testimony via video conference. When he began talking about Elvin, the boy whose funeral got him into trouble, the judge muted Ustabaş's voice. Ustabaş remains in prison. ⊗

Kaya Genç is a contributing editor for *Index on Censorship, based in Istanbul, Turkey.*

ABOVE: Mourners attend the funeral of a Turkish soldier in a terrorist attack, in Izmir, Turkey, 2018.

Rest in peace and art

Coffins in Ghana are decorated to represent the personalities of the dead. **Lewis Jennings** reports on why

47(04): 34/35 | DOI: 10.1177/0306422018819317

IN GHANA, FUNERALS are extravagant affairs: a social gathering for everyone, including extremely distant relatives and those who barely knew the deceased. And what better way to celebrate one's life than through a fantasy coffin? Coffin artists, as they are called, have developed a unique trade in parts of Ghana for *abebuu adekai*, a "proverb coffin". The flamboyant caskets, which are designed to reflect the personality or occupation of the departed, show how some Ghanaians are keen to put the "fun" into funeral. Coffins can be shaped like animals, or aeroplanes, or even a bottle of Coca Cola.

Paa Joe, a Ghanaian master craftsman, is considered one of the most important pioneers in the trade and is the subject of several documentaries covering fantasy coffins. But art curator and writer Nana Osei Kwadwo, who spoke to Joe, told Index that not everyone approved.

For a family to bury a relative in a fantasy coffin, it shows how they cherished the dead person and how gloriously they want the deceased to transition into the ancestral world

"Paa Joe told me how people were not receptive of his coffins, with some saying he's making a mockery of death," he said.

Kwadwo says many Ghanaians see death as a painful stage in life. While Kwadwo understands why fantasy coffins can be viewed as a travesty, he also believes they can be a good way for people to express emotion over the death of a loved one.

"For a family to bury a relative in a fantasy coffin, it shows how they cherished the dead person and how gloriously they want the deceased to transition into the ancestral world," he said.

Teshie-Nungua, a small town in southern Ghana, is famous for its fantasy coffin tradition. Local man Don Chikara told Index: "A chief fisherman residing along the coast, providing he's well-to-do, may want to be buried in a replica canoe coffin. Same applies to a hunter who may be buried in the belly of

a replica gun, to signify what he represented while alive.

"But take a royal, a king, for example, buried in an artsy coffin. This is usually dictated by very strict cultural and traditional rites and practices which have to be followed to the letter. There are clans with animals as their totem symbols, so if you're a king, or clan head with a 'filthy rat' as your totem, your artsy coffin will be a replica of a rat. And there, inside the belly of a rat, is exactly where your cadaver is placed before you're buried."

Taking between two and six weeks to produce, depending on the complexity of the construction and the carpenter's experience, a coffin typically costs around $400. It can be seen as a status symbol, so even though the amount is extortionate for many in Ghana, the price tag does not stop grieving families from forking out.

Chikara added: "Interestingly, the person may have been financially low on the status ladder. But, upon their death, there's often a show of affluence from the bereaved family, going to any lengths to secure a beautiful coffin. Ironically, while the deceased may have been alive and needed help, he or she may have been ignored – only for a show of affluence after their demise."

Is this something Chikara would go in for? He thinks not. "An artsy coffin for me? Not for me." ⊗

Lewis Jennings is editorial assistant at Index on Censorship

LEFT: A coffin workshop in Accra, Ghana. The Ga tribe believe a coffin should reflect the lifestyle of the deceased

When your body belongs to the state

In North Korea, there is no discussion about sex, reproduction or the human body. **Jieun Baek** discovers how this leads to disease and teenage pregnancy

47(04): 36/38 | DOI: 10.1177/0306422018819318

GROWING UP IN the North Korean border city of Hyesan, Lee Hyeon and her friends believed that if a girl merely touched a man's hand she would become pregnant.

Lee Myn, who was raised in a politically powerful family in Hamheung, the country's second largest city, was no more knowledgable.

She first learned about human reproduction during her initial year living in South Korea as an 18-year-old defector.

Lee Hyeon, now 34, and Lee Myn, 30, come from a society that does not offer sex education at school and tightly restricts the flow of information elsewhere. While anecdotes such as these might seem charmingly naive, they have very negative consequences.

Lee Myn says that when she started menstruating, she thought she was dying. Most of her female friends came to the same conclusion.

Within this environment, it's no surprise that sexually transmitted infections spread. This is particularly a problem for those who have pre-marital or extra-marital affairs. The combination of the absence of sex education, a social taboo placed on such behaviour and extremely under-resourced hospitals leads to people hiding, unintentionally spreading and not properly treating STIs. People who think they have some type of illness due to "sexually deviant" behaviour will generally be too ashamed even to seek medical treatment.

Then there's pregnancy. An unintended pregnancy out of wedlock is an issue that brings collective shame on a woman's family. Since the signs of pregnancy are not spoken of, women often don't know they are pregnant until they are quite far along. If still at school, the girl is usually expelled and left to handle her "shame" in private. Upon a quiet request, the neighbourhood's designated midwife will come to her home and carry out an abortion. In the rare instances where a child is carried to term outside marriage, the baby will be given away for adoption. It is near impossible to raise a child as a single mother.

There are several reasons why sex education might be non-existent in North Korea. It may be a hangover of the country's conservative Confucian history, a history shared with its southern counterpart prior to the peninsula's division. Until recently, South Korea was also extremely socially conservative, with premarital sex or any subject pertaining to adult bodies considered either wholly taboo or intensely awkward at best.

But North Koreans also live in a society shrouded in secrecy and are shielded from information not state approved. People are not allowed to ask for such things to be included on the curriculum as such a request would be interpreted as criticism of the state's education. Nor are they permitted to air any grievances associated with the consequences of not having proper, even minimal, sex education. There is absolutely no physical or political space

CREDIT: Ed Jones/AFP/Getty Images

for people to voice any discontent with their regime, or any extension of it, so sex education remains strictly off limits.

Lee Myn told Index that young adults engaging in these taboo behaviours, or who talk about them, are deemed "too free-spirited", "independent" and "wild", which are thinly veiled descriptions of those thought to pose moral and political threats to society.

She said: "If someone is so free with his body, then he can easily gain confidence to break the law, and be a danger in the eyes of the regime."

Indeed, the lack of sex education is as much a political issue as a personal one. Ultimately, a North Korean citizen's body belongs to the state. Citizens are not allowed to travel beyond their towns without the authorities' permission. International travel requires the regime's explicit permission and attempts to leave the nation without such permission is punishable by death.

That most North Koreans live, work and die in their home towns adds another dimension holding back the flow of information. Lee →

ABOVE: Students at a teacher training college in Pyongyang, North Korea, in 2018

Lee Myn says that when she started menstruating, she thought she was dying. Most of her female friends came to the same conclusion

If someone is so free with his body then he can easily gain confidence to break the law, and be a danger in the eyes of the regime

→ Hyeon's younger brother, Lee Seong-min, also a defector, told Index that questions of puberty, reproduction and dating were made more uncomfortable because the only people they could talk to were those they had grown up with.

"You know your peers in your home town since childhood, the same people you studied with and played with outside. Consequently, such questions and curiosities are simply not expressed. Too embarrassing."

Lee Seong-min said that when he and his classmates started getting acne and the boys' voices started sounding different, he was very confused. There was no teacher to turn to and parents did not discuss these topics with their children.

In the late-1990s, France and several other countries shipped their rubbish to North Korea and paid them to recycle it. Lee Seong-min remembers "treasure-hunting" through mountains of waste and trying to make sense of the cassette tapes, ripped clothes and sweet wrappers. He also recalls pulling out what he thought were balloons, blowing them up and playing with them with his friends. They would tie strings to the balloons and run around the streets or toss them in the air like light volleyballs. He now realises that these "balloons" were used condoms.

"How gross! But no one knew what these were. Not even the adults!" he said.

Will the situation improve? There are positive signs that it might. The wives of the first two North Korean leaders were never in the public eye. Portraying the leader as the country's father, and not the father of his immediate family, was part of constructing an image that he was living the life of highest sacrifice for the nation's citizens. This public relations strategy seems to have changed with President Kim Jong-un. His wife, Ri Sol-ju, is often seen in public, lovingly holding her husband's arm, and is present at important meetings. This may be a signal from the top that the role of women in North Korean society is changing.

Indeed, there is plenty to suggest women are gaining more of a voice in North Korean society. Since the 1990s, North Koreans have turned to small private markets to sustain themselves. While husbands would typically go to work, housewives ran these private markets. This enabled many women to bring in supplementary, and at times primary, income to their households, and from there to gain more leverage and agency.

This might help women one day to access practical and useful information on health and reproduction.

Then there is the fact that, despite the government's greatest efforts, information from the outside world does make its way into North Korea. USBs and DVDs are smuggled across the border, offering an insight into the lives of those outside the country, including their personal lives. North Koreans have reported watching Chinese and Russian movies as well as Titanic, James Bond and US soap operas, including Desperate Housewives. South Korean television dramas that have romantic scenes, though not necessarily explicitly sexual ones, are also viewed.

"North Koreans are living in what South Korea was in the 1970s; conservative, traditional and patriarchal. But North Koreans learn and adapt very quickly," said Lee Myn.

"I defected to South Korea and learned how to live in a democracy in a short period of time. Whether it's sex education, or something else, we can learn, adapt and thrive." ⊗

Jieun Baek *was born in Los Angeles. Both grandfathers fled north Korea. She is the author of North Korea's Hidden Revolution: How the Information Underground is Transforming a Closed Society*

Maternal film sparks row

In South Korea the planned film adaption of a novel about motherhood is stoking anger from men. **Steven Borowiec** finds out why

47(04): 39/41 | DOI: 10.1177/0306422018819321

A **DEBATE IS RAGING** in South Korea. Behind it: the country's most hotly disputed work of literature in recent years. The book in question, the novel Kim Ji-young Born 1982 by Cho Nam-joo, spotlights the ways in which South Korean women deal with marriage, careers and child rearing. That debate is now reaching a new level of rancour, after news broke this autumn that the book is being adapted into a movie starring prominent actress Jung Yu-mi.

Kim Ji-young Born 1982 tells the story of a 34-year-old woman who has been married for two years and is the mother of a one-year-old daughter. Kim's husband works incredibly long hours and, without her parents nearby to help, Kim gives up her job to raise the child.

At the core of the story is the main character's struggle with the reality that after a woman gives birth she has to choose between being a full-time mother and a working mother who balances her job with childcare. The second scenario is tough in South Korea, where most childcare duties fall on women's shoulders; the state-provided daycare is considered low quality, and too short to match the long hours the average Korean is expected to work. Meanwhile, according to data from the OECD, South Korean men do the least unpaid work (routine housework and taking care of household members) alongside men in Japan of the OECD countries.

Cho's novel was a huge hit, selling around one million copies. Many South Korean women saw their own lives reflected in the story, and were encouraged to talk about these issues. Until this point, these conversations rarely reached wide audiences.

But many men looked at the story and saw something different: a distorted view of South Korean society told by an entitled, whinging woman who sponges off her hardworking husband and doesn't appreciate how good she has it.

The reaction to this book is a microcosm of a loaded gender-based debate that has been bubbling for years in South Korea. In the most misogynistic corners of the Korean-language internet, full-time mothers are called "parasites" – they are accused of living lives of leisure on their husbands' earnings and the largesse of the taxpayer-funded daycare. At the same time, working mothers lament shouldering what they see as an unfair portion of child-rearing responsibilities; this limits their advancement opportunities at companies, where late-night work is common and promotion can depend on the ability to socialise with colleagues after hours.

"This generation has to work so hard every day just to survive," said Youjin Do, an author, lecturer and filmmaker in an interview with Index. "The fact is that some women become housewives even though they badly wanted to continue pursuing their careers, but their companies let them go. It's not unheard of for Korean companies to punish women who get married or become pregnant."

After the book's release, men started to complain that the story of Kim Ji-young unfairly slandered them. They lashed out at anyone who spoke favourably of the novel, or even admitted to having read it. Photos of a member of a popular K-pop girl group were burned after she mentioned having read the novel. →

Many men looked at the story and saw an entitled, whinging woman

Photos of a pop star were burned after she mentioned having read the novel

→ When Jung's casting in the main role of the film adaptation was recently announced, her Instagram page was inundated with angry comments. One man posted a petition on the website of the presidential office asking the government to block the production. "This novel presents an overly subjective viewpoint that is contrary to the gender equality South Korea should pursue," the petition reads. "If it is made into a movie, will only lead to more gender-based conflict."

As the novel's editor, Park Hye-jin feels partly responsible for the controversy. While dismayed at the contentiousness of the online debate, she says that the discourse is good for her company's bottom line. "Many people don't like the book, especially men, but whenever there's controversy, our sales increase," she told Index at the Seoul offices of Minumsa, the publishing house that released the novel. "Readers respond to the pressure by reading it more, buying copies as gifts for their friends."

One such reader is Lee Seon-mi, who is 35 and single, and works full-time in the international cooperation department of a provincial government. She describes Kim Ji-young Born 1982 as a "100% accurate" depiction of contemporary South Korean society.

Lee isn't surprised at the mixed response to the novel – that reactions to a work of literature could be so disparate, and so divided along gender lines. "Most Korean men don't think that Korean society is like this," she told Index. "Women identify with this story of a woman who has to give up her career to raise her child."

The past several decades have seen changes that have made it harder for families to raise children, Lee said. "In my mum's generation, families had many siblings, and social responsibility was shared within the family. Kids were raised by their aunts and uncles and neighbours, but society isn't like that anymore. People have to leave their hometowns to find jobs in cities, and when women have kids, they don't have networks to support them."

Against this social backdrop, fewer South Koreans are having children: the government expects the country's birth rate to fall to an all-time low of less than 1.0 in 2018, far below the replacement level of 2.1. Experts point to a matrix of reasons for this phenomenon, including the decline in stable jobs, rising property prices, and the high cost of educating and caring for children.

Another factor behind the low birth rate is a disagreement in many couples over who ought to shoulder childcare duties. "Men don't value childcare as work because they don't see it as their responsibility, they think it's women's work," said Lee Sung-hee, a lecturer in sociology and social policy at the UK's University of Derby. "And they don't have the experience of having their careers interrupted. They aren't expected to rush off in the afternoon to pick up their kids."

Kim Ji-young Born 1982 is also set to become a topic of conversation in neighbouring Japan this December, when the novel is

RIGHT: South Korean men and a woman at a traditional coming-of-age ceremony in Seoul, 2013. The ceremony reminds them of their "responsibilities" as men and women

CREDIT: Kim Hong-Ji/Reuters

published in translation. The country has similar gender and economic issues as South Korea. Park says that Minumsa is working on an English translation, though no publication date has been fixed.

In South Korea, however, the novel has touched the rawest of nerves, and the debate looks set to continue. "Women are criticised for seeking alternative lifestyles because such decisions aren't just personal – they amount to calls for substantial change to South Korea's social system," said Park. "Such calls disturb the positions of those who gain power and status from the current system. People who don't want change are quick to criticise." ⊗

Steven Borowiec *is a freelance writer based in Seoul, South Korea*

Taking Pride in change

The strict Presbytarian churches on the Scottish Isle of Lewis are losing their power, and, as **Joan McFadden** reports, that means attitudes to gay marriage are changing a little too

47(04): 42/44 I DOI: 10.1177/0306422018819322

AMANDA AND KIRSTY Maclennan are the first same-sex couple to marry in Lewis, part of the Hebrides, a far flung island group off the west coast of the Scottish mainland. They live with Kirsty's daughters Isla, 13, and Freya, 10. "We got married in 2016. There was no hassle. No issues. The lovely registrar from Harris performed the ceremony in Stornoway.

"If there was any negativity we were blissfully unaware. As for getting married in a big church? I would say we would have preferred to have got married in a church but seeing as we don't attend regularly that would just be cheek."

Although both women felt unable to come out when they were younger, by the time they got married they felt that the gossip had stopped and they were simply accepted. Around the time of their wedding there was only one hint of negativity. "When we went to get all the paperwork done, we were told that the registrar only worked part-time so we'd need to see the registrar based in Harris," said Amanda.

The Maclennans spoke to Index about attitudes to gay marriage after the Isle of Lewis held its first Pride march in October 2018, with around 500 people taking to the narrow streets. The Pride event was an open challenge to the strict Presbyterianism which has been dominant on the island for generations. Religious protestors were vocal in their opposition.

In the past, regardless of their religion or lack of it, the majority of islanders adhered to certain traditions as a way of life. This was most apparent on a Sunday, when washing would never be hung out, shops, restaurants, the golf club and sports centre were closed and the ferries and other transport stopped for the day. Over the past 20 years there have been considerable changes, including ferry sailings and shops opening, with locals making it clear that for the majority that the churches no longer hold all the power.

Last June, the Scottish Episcopal Church took the decision to allow same-sex couples to be married in church. This historic move made it the first branch of the Anglican church in the UK to allow same-sex marriage.

In May of this year, the Church of Scotland voted to draft new laws that would allow ministers to conduct same-sex marriages and the legal questions committee now has two years before it has to report back, with a final poll expected in 2021.

These other churches could be a million miles away from Lewis, where Presbyterianism dominates. There are nearly 50 churches serving a population of 20,500, of which a mere six are not Presbyterian. The churches ruling on same-sex marriage and Lewis Pride indicate that there is now much greater acceptance of gay Christians in Scotland, but in reality, although many have said it's now much easier to be gay in Lewis it's still not easy if you also profess to be a Christian.

There is no discussion in the Presbyterian churches about legalising gay marriage and it's

I'm really enjoying life now and I think I'm back in Lewis to stay, but I'm glad I left when I did. If I hadn't, I think I'd probably be married with kids now and living a lie

unlikely to happen any time soon, especially since these churches regard being gay as a sin.

Unless you've grown up in the Highlands and Islands, it's almost impossible to understand the implacable opposition to the concept of gay Christians and gay marriage.

Among the Presbyterians only essential work like caring for people or animals is done on the Sabbath and shopping, television, sport and going for a walk are all banned, with the day spent going to church, eating and reading religious books or the Bible. Preparation for Sunday starts on Saturday evening, which means any sober socialising finishing well before midnight. Sin by association is still very real. Playing sport in itself may not be sinful, but if your team competes on a Sunday then you probably shouldn't be part of it.

Against such a catalogue of potential sins, Lewis Pride didn't stand a chance of being accepted by religious leaders and their congregations. Interestingly, there was no animosity on either side of the debate, but neither was there any possibility of them meeting in the middle.

Greg MacDonald, a minister of the Free Church of Scotland (Continuing), was among religious figures who lined the route with placards carrying a biblical message. "We weren't there for confrontation but to carry the message of God," he said. "We had a prayer meeting the night before for all denominations opposed to the march and we believe that it is sending the wrong message to young people."

He added: "What they are doing is unbiblical and unpleasing to God and if anyone

came to me saying they were gay I would treat them as I would anyone else struggling with wrong sexual urges and counsel them to turn to God. Anyone can stop their behaviour with help from God."

Tabie MacDonald, who helped organise Lewis Pride, also grew up on Lewis, returning three years ago. "I started experimenting then and realised I was gay but I don't think I'd have done that if I hadn't moved away from Lewis."

"Pride opened up everyone's eyes and it helped people come to terms with their sexuality," he said. "I'm really enjoying life now and I think I'm back in Lewis to stay, but I'm →

ABOVE: Pride marchers confronted by religious protesters on the streets of Stornoway on Lewis in October 2018

glad I left when I did. If I hadn't, I think I'd probably be married with kids now and living a lie."

Lewis Pride would have been unthinkable even ten years ago, so there is hope of things changing. Tabie's mum and siblings have been totally supportive of him coming out, with his mum saying to be what you want to be and be happy. "Pride opened up everyone's eyes and it helped people come to terms with their sexuality," he said. "I'm really enjoying life now and I think I'm back in Lewis to stay but I'm glad I left when I did. If I hadn't, I think I'd probably be married with kids now and living a lie."

Even Greg MacDonald admits times are changing, in part because of the diminishing power of the church in Lewis over the last 20 years. Now ferries run on Sundays, shops are open and locals have made it clear that, for the majority, the churches no longer hold sway.

"I'm in my 40s, and when I grew up in Lewis, the churches were packed," he said. "I'm in Ness, where there are four different churches serving 1,500 people, yet on the Sabbath now

there will probably be a total of 300 in church. I think that's very sad."

He believes that plenty of gay people in Lewis didn't want to parade their sexuality through Pride. "They just want to get on and live with their neighbours in peace," he said. "I think this is more a secular push than a gay push and you can see that with who's involved – the same ones who want ferries on the Sabbath."

Lewis Pride may have been a big step forward, but the Hebrides is still a long way from Edinburgh or Glasgow – and not just geographically. ✺

Joan McFadden grew up in the Hebrides. She is a freelance journalist, based in Glasgow

SCOTTISH ATTITUDES TO SAME-SEX COUPLES

- The first same-sex marriages in Scotland took place on 31 December 2014
- Same-sex couples were allowed to adopt children on 28 September 2009
- Section 28, introduced in 1988, banned the "promotion of homosexuality". It was repealed in Scotland, England and Wales in 2000
- The Scottish National Party's 2016 manifesto supported LGBT sex education classes, including "equality training" for teachers
- LGBT-inclusive education was embedded in the Scottish school curriculum in November 2018
- A study by Time for Inclusive Education found nine in 10 LGBT Scots experienced homophobia at school, whilst 27% had reported suicide attempts after being bullied
- Scotland decriminalised homosexuality in 1980, which was 13 years later than in England and Wales
- Men who have sex with men must wait three months after having sex to donate blood
- Commercial surrogacy for gay male couples is yet to be legalised
- Lewis held its first Pride march in October 2018
- Polls conducted as part of the Scottish Social Attitudes survey found that acceptance for same-sex relationships had increased from 29% in 2000 to 59% in 2015

Lewis Jennings

What they are doing is unbiblical and unpleasing to God, and if anyone came to me saying they were gay I would treat them as I would anyone else struggling with wrong sexual urges and counsel them to turn to God

Silence about C-sections

Taboos about birthing choices mean thousands of women and babies in Nigeria die unnecessarily. **Wana Udobang** speaks to a doctor who is campaigning for change

47(04): 45/47 | DOI: 10.1177/0306422018819324

MATERNAL AND INFANT mortality rates in Nigeria are becoming a national scandal. Bill Gates has dubbed the country one of the most dangerous places in the world to have a baby, and it will be an issue in next year's presidential election.

One of the reasons for the high rates of maternal and infant death here is the taboo surrounding birth. Caesarean section rates are very low because of the stigma attached to not having a natural birth. It is also a society which does not talk about the dangers of giving birth, and still isn't investing enough money in high-quality maternity services.

C-sections, if performed properly in clean hospitals, are a way to drive down maternal mortality. A rate of 10% or higher is needed to start having an effect, but a major study published in The Lancet in 2018 found that in west and central African regions, C-sections were used in only 4.1% of births.

For most Nigerian women, marriage is a prerequisite, and having children is a rite of passage. When you are unable to give birth conventionally, it can be seen as an indictment on your womanhood, often provoking the labels "weak" and "lazy".

Many women who require C-sections during childbirth will look for hospitals or midwives, or even those who are untrained, to assist with vaginal deliveries, regardless of the risk posed to their lives and that of their unborn babies.

Abosede Lewu, an obstetrician and gynaecologist at the Lagos University Teaching Hospital, said: "In our environment, having a C-section is still seen as a form of weakness due to the combination of religion and culture. In certain cultures, if you shout during a normal delivery, you are seen as a weak woman. So the fact that you cannot do it quietly makes you a sort of failure. You can imagine with people like that, a C-section is not even an option because for you to even scream in labour, you have already dropped the baton."

Nigeria is still ranked as the country in sub-Saharan Africa with the highest rate of maternal deaths, and makes up 14% of the global maternal mortality rate. According to a Unicef report, one woman dies every 10 minutes on account of pregnancy or childbirth in Nigeria - a total of 53,000 women per year.

This parlous state of affairs was in the global spotlight in 2018 when Gates gave a speech at the National Economic Council meeting on Human Capital Investment in Abuja condemning the high infant and maternal mortality in the country. Women's representation and women's health is being highlighted by commentators as an urgent issue for the presidential elections in February 2019.

Lewu, who also runs Girls-Aid, an initiative that focuses on the wellbeing of women and girls by giving them access to health and life skills, believes that the pressure and stigma sometimes come from those closest to the mother-to-be. "There is also some kind of female bullying or peer pressure where your friends that delivered on their own sort of snigger when you have a C-section. Or →

I have a couple of friends who have had C-sections and you ask them and they still tell you that they had a vaginal delivery

ABOVE: A mother with her infant twins in a Nigerian makeshift maternity ward

→ a mother-in-law, or even a mother, to a daughter saying 'You are just lazy, you could have pushed'."

Religion is a large part of the Nigerian cultural identity, so at gatherings, weddings and even ante-natal classes it isn't out of place to hear prayers admonishing C-sections for new brides or mothers to be.

Lewu explains that this is one of the reasons women who have C-sections hide, often giving false testimonies in church about natural deliveries.

"I have a couple of friends who have had C-sections and you ask them and they still tell you that they had a vaginal delivery. It is easier for educated women who have come to terms with C-sections, but the people who contribute to maternal mortalities are the not-so-educated people," she said.

This is not just about women's choices, though. It is about a whole society which is not prepared to talk about this issue or invest properly in women's maternity services, so women are left to die because of secrecy surrounding childbirth – not only in the countryside and villages but also in cities such as Lagos.

Nigerian lifestyle vlogger Sisi Yemi vividly remembers her own birth experience three

years ago, where the women around her were unwilling to share their experiences, leaving her both anxious and confused.

"Even when you ask 'How was it for you?' they don't tell you they did the C-section, they don't tell you anything," she said. "Nobody ever talks. When I asked my friends and the people that had given birth around me, all they said was 'You will go and do your own and you will find out'."

But thanks to YouTube videos and online pregnancy apps, her anxiety didn't tip over the edge. "They tell you everything," she said. "That was where I was getting all my information from, because people around me wouldn't talk about pregnancy. Even my mother said 'Go there and experience it'."

C-sections also have a heavier cost implication, and with many Nigerians having a deep distrust of the healthcare system, there is a general belief that hospitals prioritise their bank balances over women's lives.

For Sisi Yemi, even her healthcare providers were giving less than satisfactory information, and being constantly met with a wall of silence from other women left her caught between a rock and a hard place, not knowing where to go.

"That lack of information went all the way to the end, till the delivery," she said. "They don't offer the information, so if you don't

When you are unable to give birth conventionally, it can be an indictment on your womanhood, often provoking the labels "weak" and "lazy"

know what you are asking for, you don't get the answer. They said they were going to induce me and I remember I saw something brief online about induction and I asked: 'What is this induction, is it an injection, will it be painful?'. All I was getting was typical Nigerian answers like 'don't worry'. There was no answer, really, about what the procedure was. I just knew I was going to be induced."

Women are silenced and it affects their ability to share, seek information and make informed choices about their bodies and their healthcare.

Lewu recalls a tragic incident of a woman who was booked for a C-section during her second pregnancy. Her husband – insistent that she have the baby on her own – moved her to another hospital where she ended up in labour for two days before the baby died and she needed surgery to have it taken out. She ruptured her bladder and developed infections, leading to three more surgeries and a hysterectomy.

"She was 31 and she had no baby," said Lewu. "Those are the extreme end of people that don't want a C-section."

Stigma in Nigeria is fatal. Women and society in general are not talking enough about the scandal of so many women dying in childbirth. There are many stories that range from ruptures and post-partum bleeding to deaths on a daily basis.

For Lewu, what matters is that mothers and babies survive, and this needs to trump all societal and religious dogma. ⊗

Wana Udobang *is a journalist, poet and filmmaker based in Lagos, Nigeria. She has worked with BBC Radio 4, BBC World Service and Nigeria's 92.3 Inspiration FM*

We need to talk about genocide

Abigail Frymann Rouch looks at how different nations have dealt with mass extermination, and finds out why it is so important to discuss what happened and remember the past with honesty

47(04): 48/50 I DOI: 10.1177/0306422018819326

NEXT YEAR MARKS the 25th anniversary of the Rwandan genocide, in which the country's ethnic Hutus slaughtered around 800,000 people, mostly Tutsis, in 100 days. Although plenty of survivors, politicians of the day and those responsible for the killings are still around, the details of what happened remain hotly contested.

Linda Melvern, whose third book about the genocide, Intent to Deceive, will be published in April, argues that there has been a "campaign of denial" by a network of academics, journalists, lawyers and French former military officers, intent on "minimising, distorting and altering" the facts.

"There continue to be claims of a double genocide, originally suggested by [French] President François Mitterrand in 1994," she said.

There were an estimated 30,000 reprisal killings in 1994, and she claims that "numerous attempts at moral equivalence have been made".

Genocide scholars have observed that a common feature of mass killings is not only the intention to eliminate a group of people, but also the inability, or refusal, to allow free discussion of it afterwards. So some of the most traumatic and complex episodes in a country's history become the most taboo, the most disputed or the most controlled as perpetrators and their backers defend their reputations and the status quo.

Yet the way a nation or a society faces up to such an atrocity affects how it functions in the future.

Alternative narratives about Rwanda garner eager listeners among diaspora Hutus, who blame the ruling Rwandan Patriotic Front, whose forces ended the slaughter, for their exile. However, Phil Clark, reader in comparative and international politics at SOAS University of London, believes the Rwandan government has alienated the Hutus by its tight control of the genocide narrative, especially during times of national remembrance.

"The RPF made a mistake in heavily suppressing any crimes that had been committed against the Hutus," he said. "There's no moral equivalence, but crimes against Hutus did occur, and sometimes involved the RPF. Some RPF figures admit in private that they should have acknowledged that some revenge killings took place, and should have prosecuted some RPF figures."

A law passed in 2008 banned the promotion of "genocide ideology", which Amnesty International said suppressed political dissent and freedom of speech.

Nonetheless, there is much to commend in Rwanda's handling of the aftermath, such as a Kigali Genocide Memorial Centre modelled on Israel's Yad Vashem Holocaust museum, and the establishment of community-based Gacaca courts in which hundreds of thousands of ordinary people were able to give testimony. In addition, Clark says grievances have been reduced by a socio-economic programme that has benefited Tutsi and Hutu alike.

Like the Rwandan government, the legitimacy of the post-genocide government in Cambodia rests on its overthrow of the Khmer Rouge, during whose rule, in the 1970s, about one-fifth of the population was killed or died from starvation or disease.

"Every citizen was a victim, a perpetrator, or somewhere in the grey area between the two and, especially in rural areas, people often know what their neighbours did and who they betrayed," argued Yale University anthropologist Eve Zucker.

OPPOSITE: Auschwitz survivors gather in 2018 at Birkenau camp in Poland to mark the 73rd anniversary of the liberation of the Nazi concentration and extermination camp

But the Cambodian People's Party that succeeded the Khmer Rouge has repeated the narrative that the perpetrators were Pol Pot and his closest henchmen; that lower-ranking leaders were victims themselves (many defected to the CPP); and that the authoritarian CPP, including its prime minister of 33 years, Hun Sen, a former KR battalion commander, had nothing to do with the murderous regime. Public holidays mark the overthrow of the KR and offer citizens an opportunity to express their hatred of it.

Genocide investigator and Harvard academic Craig Etcheson pointed out: "The 'big lie' technique continues to work if you repeat something over and over."

The UN-backed Khmer Rouge Tribunal, established in 1997, has tried a handful of senior, now elderly, men and two were convicted for the first time of genocide in November 2018. This validated ordinary Cambodians' experiences and made discussing them easier. Until the early 2000s Cambodians shuddered to mention the KR, because of the group's ongoing insurgency and unofficial presence in government.

The trauma of the victims has been "for the most part suppressed", Etcheson said, and even now, "most Cambodians don't trust the government, don't trust much of anybody".

This, he says, has left society atomised and riven with high levels of domestic violence, rape and gang rape. However, many young people born after the Khmer Rouge was ousted have enjoyed more education than their parents and are developing a dim view of the CPP. Over the last 11 years, the country's secondary schools have adopted a textbook, written by the Documentation Centre of Cambodia, an NGO founded by Etcheson and others, which describes the KR in academic rather than the government's terms. Zucker argues that reconciliation work by NGOs can result in former lower-level KR leaders issuing apologies and being accepted back into the community. "In some cases, their whole demeanour changes," she said, adding that others were rehabilitated after doing good deeds such as serving in Buddhist temples.

Whereas in Cambodia discussion of its genocide is increasing after decades of →

Every citizen was a victim, a perpetrator, or somewhere in the grey area between the two, and, especially in rural areas, people often know what their neighbours did and who they betrayed

The "big lie" technique continues to work if you repeat something over and over

→ government-led suppression, in Europe surely the most-analysed "genocide of genocides" is facing new challenges to the extent that it can be freely discussed.

Germany's laudable record of reconciling itself to the Holocaust is familiar: trials of senior Nazis; reparations to Israel; museums; city-centre memorials; Chancellor Willy Brandt kneeling outside the site of the Warsaw Ghetto uprising in 1970. Schoolchildren visit concentration camps and plaques have been put up outside victims' homes. The Germans even developed a word, *Vergangenheitsbewältigung*, for "coming to terms with the past", but that wasn't always easy.

"In West Germany, you had lots of ex-Nazis who quickly found themselves in the government of West Germany," said William Schabas, professor of international law at Middlesex University. "[In Soviet-controlled East Germany,] there wasn't as much free speech ... and there was also a kind of smug satisfaction that they were pro-Soviet, they were the people who had defeated the Nazis."

Not that East Germans did not need to come to terms with what had gone before. Elke Schwarz,who grew up in West Germany and lectures in political theory at Queen Mary's, London, said the fall of the Berlin Wall in 1989 pushed East Germans to come to terms with the surveillance, violence and depression that had become endemic.

Today, the far-right Alternative für Deutschland is the largest opposition party in the German parliament and, says Schwarz, its rhetoric rejects the *Vergangenheitsbewältigung* legacy in favour of a nostalgia for military prowess and a "mysticism about the good old days".

The records of Germany's neighbours have also been mixed. In January, amid the rising tide of nationalism in eastern Europe, Poland was criticised for a step it took to emphasise its wartime suffering and play down any complicity. Under its socially conservative right-wing Law and Justice (PiS) government, MPs passed a law prohibiting anyone from accusing the Polish state or Polish nation of being responsible or complicit in Nazi crimes, and advocating fines or prison sentences for those found guilty.

Poland rejects the term "Polish death camps" because the camps on its soil were Nazi-run. Six million Poles, of whom half were Polish Jews and half non-Jewish Poles, were murdered in Nazi-run camps. But Israeli Prime Minister Benjamin Netanyahu was furious with the new law and described it as an "attempt to rewrite history". In June, an amendment was passed to downgrade penalties to civil offences.

Nowhere is the fight for Poland's war narrative more clearly seen than at the Gdansk Museum of the Second World War, which opened in 2017 after being commissioned by the former prime minister Donald Tusk. The current PiS government has found it "not Polish enough" – its founding curator was removed and some of the exhibits were changed.

So genocide can be followed by the denial of the crimes committed, or of some of the grey areas around them. While eliminating hate speech is important for stability, honest discussion and exploration of events are necessary for a society's longer-term functioning.

Paul Roth, professor of philosophy at the University of California, Santa Cruz, says that societies with just one received narrative of events tend to cope badly if that narrative is challenged, and they are "more brittle". The emergence of new nationalisms, and terms such as "post-truth" and "fake news", show that maintaining accurate and fair narratives is an ongoing task. ⊗

Abigail Frymann Rouch is a freelance journalist, based in London, specialising in religious affairs and human rights

Opposites attract ... trouble

It is 70 years since the Prohibition of Mixed Marriages Act, but in post-apartheid South Africa, author **Bhekisisa Mncube** says relationships across the race divide are still difficult

47(04): 51/53 | DOI: 10.1177/0306422018819328

WHEN IT COMES to marriage, I jumped off the cliff: I married a white woman. In marrying a white woman, I consciously crossed the colour line and, in the process, mixed bodies and cultures. As we know, interracial intimate relationships continue to be fraught with peril around the globe. In the case of South Africa, this is despite the post-apartheid constitution that guarantees equal rights and forbids racism.

My relationship with my English wife began years after the removal from our statutes of this law (repealed in 1985) and the two other laws that made interracial intimate relationships a criminal act: the Immorality Amendment Act, 1957 (repealed in 1985) and the Group Areas Act, 1950 →

ABOVE: Author Bhekisisa Mncube whose marriage to a white woman caused a stir in his family

→ (repealed in 1990). However, in spite of a favourable legal framework, an intimate interracial relationship in a socially stratified society such as South Africa isn't always champagne and roses. I have come face to face with racial prejudice and racial discrimination. In our 17 years of courtship and marriage, our relationship continues to cause a stir – and this isn't likely to change for years to come.

At first, one of my wife's long-time friend's called our union "the biggest mistake". Being referred to in this way still hurts today, as it did then. Unsurprisingly, she wasn't a lone wolf – my own people (read: blacks) had a mouthful to say. I am a traitor; I will increase, through birth, another race, different from mine – coloureds, so the line went.

The hurtful word "coloured" pierces my heart every day. Strangely, it comes from friends, foes and strangers alike. Most of these comments about breeding another race came from black people. In their racial thinking, I have committed the ultimate crime – a crime of passion across the colour line. I am effectively sleeping with the enemy. It is a pedantic detail that our relationship occurred deep into post-apartheid South Africa.

It is argued that opposition to interracial intimate relationships may indicate what Professor Kapano Ratele, of the Institute for Social and Health Sciences at the University of South Africa, has named "subtle racism". At its core, this new form of racism is no less racist or offensive than "old-fashioned" racism; it is just disguised in a more sophisticated and socially accepted argument – that of opposition to intimate relationships between people classified as belonging to different racial groups. Justifications for this opposition are based on supposedly non-racist reasons, such as concern for the welfare of the children produced by such relationships.

I even lost a close friend who, unbeknown to me, was entangled in a fantasy love affair with me. She didn't hold back, saying: "I can't be friends with you now that you're dating a white woman. I simply can't go on and be with you while you're dating whites."

I was stunned. I had no idea that, firstly, she was a racist and, secondly, she was emotionally invested in our friendship. Over the years, I have lost more friends than I care to count.

Sadly, not even Durban – where we lived then – was ready for an interracial couple walking the streets, chatting, kissing and holding hands with gay abandon.

Many a time, we got hostile stares and suffered outright prejudice. I recall walking into a restaurant once, holding hands, and sitting ourselves down. Seconds, then minutes, passed. Nobody brought us menus. Nobody took our our drinks order. Nobody bothered to tell us we were not welcome. We had to figure out that we had touched a raw nerve of whiteness and its bedfellows, prejudice and naked racism. We never set foot in that establishment again. I am thankful that restaurant didn't last long.

However, intimate interracial relationships are inherently intricate. In my case, the issue of cultural differences runs too deep. I am Zulu by birth; she is English. I am a carnivore; she is a vegetarian. I believe in sorceresses and ancestors; she doesn't. She is a non-practising Catholic; I am non-practising believer in uMvelinqangi, the African god of creation. These differences have far-reaching consequences. For instance, to appease my parents after our wedding, I suggested a traditional wedding at which we would slaughter a cow to introduce the new bride to the ancestors. My wife does not believe in animal slaughter on principle. Obviously, she doesn't want to be associated with the willy-nilly slaughter of animals in her name. She refused. The stalemate continues: my parents continue to push for the traditional wedding, in vain. I have decided to choose my wife over my parents.

Despite this traditional wedding hiatus, my family has long accepted my white wife. Two years ago, my father relented and introduced my English wife to our Zulu ancestors without the compulsory slaughter of any domestic animal. My mother speaks only words of kindness about her. She is regarded as an important member of the Mncube family. I am also fortunate in that my English wife's family has accepted me and my Zuluness. In an interview for my book, my mother-in-law said: 'So much joy from watching the two of you grow and mature together. It needed a strong love bond to make a success of a mixed-race marriage, and you can be proud."

There is a light at the end of the tunnel, as new research on intimate interracial relationships shows that racial polarisation is narrowing. A 2011 study conducted by Acheampong Yaw Amoateng, a research professor of sociology and family studies at North-West University in Mafikeng, on interracial marriages provided good news. Researchers examined the likelihood of South Africans marrying outside their race, as well as the factors influencing interracial marriages. The study showed that, in 1996, the chance of someone marrying

I can't be friends with you now that you're dating a white woman. I simply can't go on and be with you while you're dating whites

outside his or her race was 303:1. In 2011, the chance had increased to 95:1. While marrying within one's race is still the norm in South Africa, studies show that this is slowly starting to change. And groups who have previously been found least likely to marry outside their race – Asians, Indians and whites – are increasingly choosing partners of another race. A recorded 5% of coloureds, Asians and Indians chose interracial marriage, while whites were the least likely among all races to do so. The most common interracial marriage is between blacks and coloureds. Black men are the most likely to marry outside their race while black women are least likely.

Fourteen years ago, we were blessed with a beautiful daughter named Miss N. Three years ago, she told me she had resolved the issue of her racial identity, saying: "Dad, I am a suburban Zulu girl."

She will have nothing to do with the apartheid-inspired political identity of mixed-race South Africans being coloureds. It is therefore my contention that we need to reimagine the tired concepts of apartheid-fuelled race identity and racial profiling. While intimate interracial relationships aren't a piece of cake in a racially polarised society, it is a journey that we have found liberating and life-affirming. After all, we are human beings before the socially constructed notion of race. Let us love and let us live. ⊛

Bhekisisa Mncube lives in Pretoria, South Africa, and is the director of speechwriting for the minister of basic education. He is the author of The Love Diary of a Zulu Boy (Penguin Random House)

GLOBAL VIEW

My year in review: snowflakes and diamonds

Contrary to some people's expectations, under-18s are happy to stand up for free speech, and for those with whom they disagree, says **Jodie Ginsberg**

47(04): 54/55 | DOI: 10.1177/0306422018819329

AT A SPEECH on media freedom recently, a fellow panellist asked if I was going to be able to say anything optimistic. Small wonder: it has been a grim year for democracy. We are bombarded on a daily basis with stories that illustrate starkly the closure of spaces for civic and civil discourse – from the attacks on journalists and journalism in countries from the USA to Hungary to the heated and ugly debate on transgender issues both online and off.

The coarsening of public debate has thrown into sharp relief the question of the role that freedom of expression plays in such an environment. Is it enabling hate or promoting tolerance? And in such a febrile environment it is little surprise that calls are growing for certain groups and ideas to be denied space. Blame for this notion (that a whole raft of issues should simply no longer be discussed) is often laid at the door of young people, dismissively referred to as the "snowflake generation". But this year has convinced me that the snowflake narrative is overdone. In fact, the people with whom I have had the most robust, open-minded discussions about the value of free speech have been

under-18s. Which means I am able to speak with a degree of optimism.

Two events in particular struck a chord with me this year – a year that marks 50 years since the 1968 protests, many led by students, that heralded international social change. The first was an English National Opera youth camp for students from diverse backgrounds. The students, aged from 13 to 18, spent a week devising a show on issues of censorship. I led a workshop that covered issues such as drill music, homophobia and racism and, instead of the vehement defences of censorship I expected, I was bowled over by the nuanced, critical thinking evinced by this group of teenagers.

Instead of the militant defence of a position we are so used to seeing when engaged in debates – on social media in particular, or when watching most TV news debates – participants were respectful, willing to challenge and be challenged, and, crucially, willing to listen to other points of view and shift stance.

The students discussed recent examples of censorship in the UK including the dropping of "human zoo" performance Exhibit B from a planned staging at The Barbican; the cancelling of Homegrown, a play about radicalisation by the National Youth Theatre; and music bans. "We talked a lot about censorship and self-censorship," said one of the students, who admitted he hadn't given much thought to self-censorship and how it influenced his own personal interactions before the programme. After it, he said he realised "creators are people still censored even in our democratic society".

I experienced much the same level of thoughtfulness and enthusiasm at a workshop

No one shouted. No one stormed off in a huff (actual or virtual)

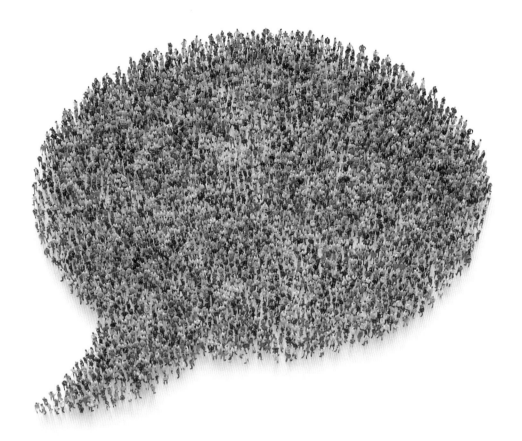

later in the year with a group of school-age children in Brisbane, whom I tasked with identifying topics they deemed "taboo" and explaining why. Far from the arguments I expected – that x and x issue is taboo because it is simply "no longer up for discussion" and "that battle has been won" (often articulated by much older, and supposedly wiser, critics of free speech) – I again heard a group actively wrestling to understand why certain issues had been deemed off limits for discussion and what this meant for society.

I then asked the students to adopt a position they disagreed with and to argue that position to someone else. I expected silence. Instead, I heard and witnessed earnest attempts to understand ideas that for many were beyond the pale. No one shouted. No one stormed off in a huff (actual or virtual). No one resorted to verbal abuse. Some of the discussions were uncomfortable, but the discourse was respectful, thoughtful and earnest throughout.

Yes, there is plenty to worry about in modern discourse. Contemporary media, from television to Twitter, encourages us to see debate as necessarily polarised. And there are plenty of factors that have encouraged that. But the experience of working with young people has left me energised and optimistic. Young people are not all snowflakes. In my experience there is a group hungry to understand the world and make sense of it through robust and respectful debate. In that sense they are far more like those other structures of glittering, crystalline beauty: diamonds. And just as hard. ⊗

Jodie Ginsberg *is the Index CEO*

IN FOCUS

58 KILLING THE NEWS? RYAN MCCHRYSTAL
Photographer Paul Conroy reveals why the
future of war reporting is looking bleak

61 AN UNDELIVERED LOVE LETTER
JEMIMAH STEINFELD
Kite Runner star Khalid Abdalla is fighting
the Egyptian censorship board to get his film
about the Arab Spring screened

64 CHARACTER (F)LAWS ALISON FLOOD
Peter Carey, Francine Prose, Mark Haddon
and Melvin Burgess discuss whether their
acclaimed books could be published today

68 MAKE ART NOT WAR LAURA SILVIA BATTAGLIA
Activists in Yemen are expressing their
resistance against war using street art

71 TRUTH OR DARE SALLY GIMSON
Nobel Prize-winning author Svetlana
Alexievich speaks about threats to her

**73 FROM ARMED REBELLION TO
RADICAL RADIO** STEPHEN WOODMAN
New Year's Day will mark the 25th anniversary
of the Zapatista uprising in Mexico, now the
movement runs a radio station and schools

Killing the news

Photographer **Paul Conroy**, who was working with Sunday Times war correspondent Marie Colvin when she was killed in Syria, tells **Ryan McChrystal** about his fears for war reporting in the years to come

47(04): 58/60 I DOI: 10.1177/0306422018819330

THE SEVEN-YEAR-LONG SYRIAN civil war has brought a new reality: a situation so dangerous that editors who once gave carte blanche to journalists covering war zones have become reluctant to send any at all – and not just to Syria, says photographer Paul Conroy.

"Everyone is out to get you in one way or another," Conroy, who worked for many years alongside Sunday Times reporter Marie Colvin, told Index, following a screening of Under the Wire, a new documentary about the pair's work in Syria.

When Colvin was killed, and Conroy was injured in a rocket attack by the Bashar al-Assad regime on 22 February 2012, the war was still in its opening months, but the face of war reporting had already changed.

"There was a massive reaction to Marie's killing," said Conroy. "I was at a lot of meetings with editors and all of a sudden it went from journalists doing pretty much what we wanted to everybody becoming a lot more security-aware. It stopped the flow of news for quite a long time."

But it isn't just the regime that has editors shaken up. For one, journalists can fetch a hefty ransom for kidnappers.

"It used to be the case that you'd run around with a big 'PRESS' sticker on your car, but I don't think that's going to help you any more," he said. "Now you may as well run around with an ATM sign on your head.

"Then we got into the beheadings of mates of mine, Jim Foley and Steven Sotloff," he added, referring to two journalists murdered by Isis. Video footage of their executions shocked the world. "The whole tone of everything changed."

Conroy says the press preoccupation with Isis coupled with a dearth of Western reporters on the ground seemed like good news for the Syrian government. "While they were doing that, Assad carried on with the same process of bombing the place to rubble."

The dictator, however, has not been entirely successful at controlling the war's narrative. "Silencing the press only made a certain amount of people more determined," said Conroy. "When Marie was killed, the world's press instantly focused on Syria It brought more attention than he would like.

"The cabal that runs Syria lives in a bubble. Assad's dad got away with murder in Hama in '82. They crushed the place, and barely a photograph exists of what happened. So this is a family trait. Assad is thinking 'He got away with it and so can I'. But it has backfired for him because he immediately came under scrutiny."

Still, the difficulties in reporting can't be ignored. Even if a Western editor were willing to send a journalist into Syria, the same journey that Conroy and Colvin made – crawling half-bent through a 3km storm drain having been passed around various unknown figures in the dark – is no longer an option.

"We relied so much on goodwill," said Conroy. "The Arab Spring had happened and the people who had taken us in and out all had a sense of optimism that things were about to change for the better. We reaped the benefits and we knew they'd look after us."

One such person was their Syrian translator and fixer Wa'el, who now lives in Finland. "He was the linchpin," said Conroy. "Before him, we were travelling blind. Once we met him it was like the lights had come on. His English was impeccable and he didn't want any money, he just wanted to be part of the revolution."

People like Wa'el are hard to come by and don't get the praise they deserve, Conroy says. "Without him, we'd all be dead."

CREDIT: Paul Conroy

ABOVE: Reporter Marie Colvin (centre) in Baba Amr, Homs, Syria, shortly before she was killed

Such benevolence no longer exists. "Journalists have been going in for seven years, and the Syrians are now asking 'what are you doing here? You keep coming but the world has done nothing. We've been shafted'."

Conroy says he would "very seriously think twice" about entering Syria today. He was able to tell from his time in the Royal Artillery that the Baba Amr Media Centre, an apartment in a partly bombed building in the south-west of Homs, where Colvin was killed, wasn't collateral damage and that the regime intended to kill the journalists. The bombers were using a military technique called "bracketing". This is when soldiers adjust their shelling until they hit their intended target. A claim brought by Colvin's sister, Cathleen, to a Washington court in April 2018 also presented evidence that the Syrian government had "assassinated" the journalist.

Even before they entered Syria, Lebanese intelligence had informed the pair that if "any Western journalist was found in Homs they would be executed and thrown on the battlefield".

It has become accepted, somewhere in the ether, to attack journalists. We are now their prey. We are fair game

"It's astonishing to see the levels the regime was prepared to go to silence the press," Conroy said. "You're now more in danger with a camera than a rifle."

The Syrian government was very aware of the power of the media when it decided to attack Homs, he added. "The last thing they wanted was civilian or foreign journalists in the place. There was a lot of time, effort and money spent on tracking equipment and units to track down journalists."

Around 400,000 people have died so far in the Syrian conflict, including at least 241 media workers, according to Reporters Without Borders. The last two Western reporters to be killed were Foley and Sotloff in 2014. While the overall number of media workers to lose their lives has steadily declined between 2013 (67) and 2017 (13), this does not mean there has been a matched decline in brutality. Rather, it is a sign of how few foreign reporters are now willing to travel to the country.

"I know for a fact that Syrian activists and journalists are still being killed. That has never stopped," said Conroy.

The photographer had worked with Colvin on many assignments since they met in

ABOVE: Photographer
Paul Conroy on
assignment in Libya
with correspondent
Marie Colvin

work in the dark.
They really don't
like people like us
snooping about, but
that's what she was
driven by."

The story that
got Colvin noticed
by the regime was
her coverage of the
widows' basement
in Homs, a place
where women
and children took
refuge but a place
the Syrian govern-
ment claimed was
a hideout for ter-
rorists. "Marie was
able to take their
stories and really
deliver something
that made the
world look. She
wanted to be the
world's eyes in these dark places."

Conroy says that he and Colvin "were
almost the last of that generation, where we
would be given a big pile of money and go
there for as long as they wanted and pretty
much do what we wanted". And the effects
have been widespread.

In 2013, a friend of Conroy's working for
The Sunday Times was travelling to cover a
story in the Central African Republic. "He got
on a flight in Nairobi, and by the time he'd
landed he had a message telling him to come
back because it was too dangerous." News
editors and security issues will restrict reporting
in the future, he said

"I hope I'm wrong, but I don't see how
things like this go back. It has become accepted,
somewhere in the ether, to attack journalists.
We are now their prey. We are fair game." ⊗

*But it isn't just the regime
that has editors shaken up...
journalists can fetch a hefty
ransom for kidnappers*

→ 2003. "Marie was notoriously bad at working with photographers, so The Sunday Times
couldn't believe it when we were still together
after a week," Conroy said. "We discovered
that we both wanted to tell the same story,
which was that these smart bombs and bullets
flying about aren't all that smart."

Colvin didn't enjoy the frontline, Conroy
explained, adding: "She wouldn't have known
a Lancaster Bomber from a Mig. She wasn't
interested in the big military picture or what
weapons or tanks were being used. Her focus
was on people." And that made her dangerous.

"These regimes, like [Muammar] Qaddafi
and Assad, going back many years, like to

Ryan McChrystal *is assistant online editor
at Index on Censorship*

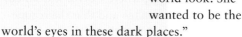

CREDIT: Paul Conroy

An undelivered love letter

A film about the Egyptian Arab Spring is winning international plaudits, but still cannot be seen in the country it wants to appeal to the most. **Jemimah Steinfeld** talks to actor and producer **Khalid Abdalla**

47(04): 61/63 I DOI: 10.1177/0306422018819331

KHALID ABDALLA IS frustrated. The British-Egyptian actor, best known for his roles in Hollywood blockbusters like United 93, the Kite Runner and the Green Zone, has come up against a brick wall. The Egyptian censors have banned his cherished film about the Arab Spring, which he produced and in which he plays a starring role.

Formally released a little over a year ago, In the Last Days of the City has garnered awards around the world. The film is set in Cairo in the two years which preceded the revolution of 2011.

But it has not found favour in the country to which it was dedicated. It was pulled from the Cairo International Film Festival and is currently banned in Egypt.

"We have an ongoing court case against the censorship board, and we'll see where that takes us. [The trial date] keeps moving – that's part of the way it works," Abdalla said.

Asked whether they would show the film surreptitiously, to an invitation-only audience in a private venue, he responds with a firm "No – it would be too much of a risk."

"The laws right now are Draconian and they can be dangerous if you break them. So doing something like that would be a liability," he told Index.

Instead, they are fighting within the legal system "because part of our struggle is not to be pushed outside spaces that we should have a right to be in".

In the meantime, they satisfy themselves with screenings outside Egypt, such as the sell-out one Index attended recently in London, at Arab arts centre the Mosaic Rooms.

The day after the screening, Abdalla said it was "incredibly painful" not being able to show the film in Cairo, "in the city that it's so clearly a love letter to".

Conceived in 2006, the film took around a decade to make. Slow and melancholy in →

RIGHT: A still from In the Last Days of the City, a film about the years running up to the Egyptian revolution and starring Khalid Abdalla

We shot it before things exploded, we finished it as they exploded, we edited it during the heyday of the revolution and we continued editing as the revolution turned to counter-revolution, and we finished it when the counter-revolution became a new order

→ nature and featuring documentary footage of Cairo, it follows the narrative of aspiring filmmaker Khalid, played by Abdalla. In between shots within shots, you see him with his friends, his ex-girlfriend and his unwell mother, and embarking on the mundane task of finding a new apartment.

What exactly riled the censors? As Abdalla says, the film is a love letter to Cairo. And with films such as Clash – a fictional take on real-life protesters across the country being forcibly taken into vans where many were never seen again – being shown in Egypt, it's not obvious

why Abdalla's film became movie non-grata. Abdalla can only speculate.

"The film was made legally with the knowledge of the authorities," he said. "That's not to say that that was an easy process to get it made. But it was also made under one political circumstance and it was released under another political circumstance. It's arguable as to whether that issue would have been there or not had there not been a revolution – there might very well have been the same problems."

Perhaps it is the signs of discontent, which boil beneath the surface like a volcano ready to erupt, such as scenes of workers striking, Islamist marches and police brutality. At the Mosaic Rooms screening, Abdalla told the audience that it captured elements of "a kind of slow war, if you want to call it that, where you end up having buildings destroyed, you end up with thousands of people dying, you end up with the slow manifestations of war. We didn't know obviously that things would explode later".

He added: "We finished filming six weeks before the revolution in Egypt broke out… We shot it before things exploded, we finished it as they exploded, we edited it during, if you like, the heyday of the revolution and we continued editing as the revolution turned to counter-revolution, and we finished it when the counter-revolution became a new order. Throughout that period the footage kept reflecting different intensities."

What's the situation like now for filmmakers in Egypt? Abdalla says it has become much more difficult to work there, although it's not completely lights out for the industry.

"It's a lot harder

being on the streets of Cairo now with a camera than it was and it's harder to get permission to film. And beyond the relationship with the authorities, there's also a much greater social mistrust here of the camera than there was," he said, adding: "There were times when literally just putting up your mobile phone could attract attention from anyone, and particularly the authorities."

He concludes he probably couldn't make In the Last Days of the City now. "You could make other films which are worth making and indeed are being made, but it's a lot harder.

"There has been a massive decrease in the amount of films being made, there has been a closing down of spaces, there has been a kind of de-facto expulsion of people – not a direct one, but you know if you can't do what you want to do then it makes you leave…"

Given this, he's not hopeful for the immediate future, saying that people's artistic capacity is "severely limited and restricted". But nor has he completely abandoned all optimism.

"What I am hopeful about is the way in which these last 10 years have oriented people's minds and experiences and what that will produce in various different cultural and artistic forms," he said.

If anything, this film is a case in point. "It was a film that built other spaces," he explained. One of these spaces is the Mosireen collective in Cairo, which Abdalla helped found in 2011. Made up of a group of revolutionary filmmakers and activists, Mosireen is dedicated to supporting citizen media across Egypt. Three months after it began, it became the most watched non-profit YouTube channel in Egypt. In January 2012, it took the title of most watched globally.

For Abdalla, while Egyptian filmmakers currently struggle with the blunt end of censorship, there are other, subtler, silencing tactics at work. He says that people "tend to think of censorship at the end of it", adding: "The most powerful form of censorship is infrastructural because it begins to seep into your imagination as well, and censorship of your imagination is the point at which you go 'well, it's impossible to make it, or if we make it no one will ever see it, so why

bother?' and that has an incredible sway on what stories do end up being told and not."

Abdalla says this is a problem Western film studios share, of which he has extensive experience.

"A big part of me wanting to do a story in Egypt is that there are stories you cannot tell about other parts of the world in Western cinema broadly speaking, whether that's European or American," he said.

"You can't tell them, they will never be funded, the stories are considered not to appeal to people and you end up with either a kind of parochial view of elsewhere or a version of elsewhere that fits your idea of how it makes you comfortable to believe that it is. And the obvious manifestations of that are stereotypes.

"From the perspective of you wanting to work, and wanting a career that's fulfilling in which there are the roles available, every minority – not just Arabs, women as well – are in that struggle to change the ground on which you can tell stories."

The ground is certainly shifting, though not always in the most positive direction. At least when it comes to In the Last Days of the City, the film has been made and the story is slowly being told. It just needs to be screened in Egypt. ⊗

Jemimah Steinfeld *is deputy editor of Index on Censorship*

ABOVE: Tahrir Cinema: people on Cairo's Tahrir Square in 2011 watching videos of the revolution **LEFT**: Khalid Abdalla in a shot from the film

Character (f)laws

Fiction writers increasingly face controversy if they write about characters who don't reflect their personal experience. **Alison Flood** asks four authors if they think they could publish their acclaimed books today

47(04): 64/67 I DOI: 10.1177/0306422018819342

KEIRA DRAKE, THE author of young adult novel The Continent, found herself rewriting the story after early reviews slammed its "white saviour" narrative earlier this year.

Drake worked on her new draft with "sensitivity readers", to whom publishers are increasingly turning in order to vet manuscripts for, as the Writing in the Margins database puts it, "internalised bias and negatively charged language". They also look at "issues of representation" across fields from disability to – as in Drake's case – race.

Writers and publishers tread a thorny path between the vital drive for more diverse representation in literature and the charged atmosphere online, where public outcry follows accusations of cultural appropriation.

Does this mean that novelists shouldn't tackle "other" voices? Does it mean that acclaimed titles of the past would be received differently today? ⊗

Alison Flood is a freelance writer

FRANCINE PROSE

Blue Angel

FRANCINE PROSE, NOVELIST and former president of the PEN American Center, had the disconcerting experience of being able to see exactly what would happen if her novel Blue Angel, which was nominated for the National Book Award and published to great acclaim in 2000, were to be submitted to publishers today. A film based on the book, Submission, was released this year: "Movie About Student-Teacher Affair Fails Gender Politics 101," screamed the headline in Rolling Stone in response.

"It's about a college professor who falls in love with a student. The novel got very well received here and did really well and then the film came out ... [It] was just shredded because it was perceived to have come out on the wrong side of the #MeToo movement. And it was the same story as the novel, essentially," Prose said. "There were a number of reviews that made me sound like I was some right-wing anti-feminist nutjob when, in fact, nothing could be further from the truth. It was very weird."

Prose believes the reaction of publishers would have been completely different if she had submitted it today. "One of the reasons the novel resonated when it came out was that people recognised that these things happened. I think now people seem to think if they do happen they only happen a certain way – which I don't believe. They're not always cases of predation. They can be love affairs gone very badly with a power differential. Those are two very different things," she said.

"And let me just say – and I really need to be clear in these situations – I am very much on the side of the #MeToo movement. I don't believe that rapists should be allowed to wield power over women in the workplace but that's not, in fact, what happens in my novel. [Reviewers today] can't even see the young woman has power, although it's perfectly clear. All they see is 'older professor has affair with younger student equals predator'."

MELVIN BURGESS

Junk

MELVIN BURGESS IS the Carnegie Medal-winning author of the controversial young adult novel Junk, which deals with drug addiction.

"Junk was shocking back in the day because YA wasn't a recognised form [of literature] in this country at the time... These days it wouldn't cause such a stir and I like to think it would be taken up pretty quickly," he said. "If I were to pick books that might struggle it would be the more experimental ones, the oddities, such as Lady: My Life as a Bitch, or Sara's Face." The former sees a teenager turned into a dog, the latter is a creepy thriller about plastic surgery.

"YA commands big sales now and I don't think publishers are so willing to take risks and get books out there that might not sell so well. Mind, I'm talking about the big publishers now – there are plenty of smaller ones who publish for the love of books rather than just for profit. It's definitely the smaller outfits that grow talent and aren't so ruled by profit and loss," said Burgess. He has just published a new novel, The Lost Witch and has been unable to find a publisher for his memoir about his own teenage years.

"When it got turned down, I had all sorts of people knocking at my door asking for the film rights and so on, on the grounds that, since I wrote it, it would be a great heap of sin and degradation. But nothing could be further from the truth. Like a lot of teens, I had a fairly boring adolescence and it was only in my twenties that I was able to really jump in the deep end. I don't know if it would be published today. Maybe I'll dig it out one day and see."

Burgess is clear that authors should be able to write characters who don't reflect their own identities. "In fact, I'm doing just that right now. The reason is that if we're going to have diversity, we white cis writers need to be able to do that. It's not easy – people from minorities are surrounded by people like me, whereas I only get to know occasional pools of them. They know us but we don't know them. I appreciate that own voices are the more important ones, but if you're a novelist you need to be able to give voice to all sorts of characters and reflect or cogitate on the society you live in. Otherwise, what's the point?"

PETER CAREY

||||||||||||||||||||||||||||||||||||||||||||||||||||||||||||||||||||||||||||||||||||||

A Long Way From Home

THE DOUBLE BOOKER Prize-winning novelist Peter Carey tackled Australia's thorny relationship with its past in his latest novel, A Long Way From Home, and admits that he had some concerns as he started writing.

"When I began A Long Way from Home, my friends feared for me. I feared for myself a little, too, but I took the time and trouble to show respect, to share both drafts and final manuscripts, to invite participation and criticism – all things that make the final draft richer, truer, but never tame," he said.

For many years, Carey has sought out "people whose special expertise is seldom literary" with whom to share his late drafts.

"I always approach this apprehensively and, of course, discover I have been totally wrong about all sorts of things, from flying Bleriot monoplanes to riding horses [and] the possibility of a piano in a Penang brothel. 'Impossible,' my experts say. 'Could never happen.' Am I stupid to make myself so vulnerable? Do I allow myself to be censored by people who read airport thrillers? The opposite. These early readers, like all readers, become the writer's collaborators, and what I end up with, far from being diminished, is a truer, more complex imagining which I would never have had without their help," he said.

So he trusted to this experience "when I came to write about the cruelties of British invasion of what we call Australia; the lingering damage still felt by Aboriginals; and the continuing injustice administered by white society", and set out to "get to know my Aboriginal neighbours".

"I did this in person, by email, with frequent flyer miles, on the phone from New York to north-west Australia, in conversations with close to 50 individuals, white and black," he said. "I learned and listened. I had some dialogue corrected and other lines rewritten by a teacher of Creole. After these glorious improvements, I shared my last two drafts with two gifted Aboriginal writers who would be quick to tell me if I was making a dick of myself."

He says he "did OK, it seems", and publishers jumped on the latest novel from the two-time Booker winner. But he passes on "one simple tip" to those who might follow: "Always spell Aboriginal with a capital A – same as the A in Australian and the E in English."

He added: "Many of my white friends cautioned me against putting my nose where it did not belong. Yet, as I kept on telling them, this was a white story, too. None of these atrocities would have occurred without white people. It seemed cowardly not to own the truth. "This is why I write, because it is a writer's job, in my opinion, to imagine what it is to be someone else."

CREDIT: (Carey) Laura Wilson; (Haddon) Charles Moriarty

> *Many of my white friends cautioned me against putting my nose where it did not belong*

MARK HADDON

The Curious Incident of the Dog in the Night-Time

" **I DON'T THINK THERE'S** anything I wrote, or wanted to write, that might not (or should not) get published today. But The Curious Incident of the Dog in the Night-Time was banned on various occasions in the US, which was interesting in various ways. And of course some people still consider it offensive because I'm not on the spectrum," said British author Mark Haddon of his award-winning and bestselling mystery novel, which is narrated by a boy with Asperger's.

"Every so often I hear complaints about Curious Incident from people who identify as being on the autistic spectrum themselves, or who are close relatives of people who identify as being on the autistic spectrum. They usually fall into two categories: one, that my portrayal of Christopher is stereotypical and reductive; two, that I should not have written the book because I am not, myself, someone who identifies as being on the autistic spectrum. The latter critics sometimes describe me [as] making money from the experience of people like themselves."

Haddon has much to say in response. First, there's the other side of the picture: he has also been "contacted by a significant number of readers who have said that the book describes their lives with uncanny accuracy". Second, he reveals that Christopher was not intended specifically to be a character on the autistic spectrum. "I put him together by combining traits, behaviours, beliefs and tics which I drew from a number of people I knew, none of whom would regard themselves as having any kind of 'learning difficulty' or 'developmental disorder' (I'm using those quote marks very deliberately)," said Haddon. "Indeed, the title essays which punctuate the narrative are, in one sense, me simply indulging myself and talking to camera. I simply intended to create an interesting, empathetic, quirky, believable character. And there is a profoundly important issue here. There is nothing fundamental which separates Christopher from the rest of us. Very few readers don't share something with Christopher. It is the combination of traits, behaviours, beliefs and tics which creates great difficulties for him and his family."

Should he not have written the book because he does not identify as being on the autistic spectrum, he wonders? "That phrase, 'on the autistic spectrum', suggests that this is a very well-defined group of people. However, the definition itself is contentious, the borderlines are very fuzzy indeed, and the 'disorder' is characterised by a number of features which can be present or not to different degrees," he said.

"I have met people who define themselves as being on the autistic spectrum who appear to have nothing in common with one another. I have also met many people in my life who exhibit a number of those features, but who would never think of themselves as being on the autistic spectrum. In short, how 'like Christopher' would one have to be to qualify as being able to write his story (noting in passing that if you were genuinely 'like Christopher' you would find the idea of writing a novel inconceivable)? Does the fascination with mathematics and science which I share with Christopher not count? Or must I have similar difficulties with social interactions? And if so, why is the latter considered more important than the former? Christopher would think the former far more important than the latter."

Every so often I hear complaints about Curious Incident from people who identify as being on the autistic spectrum themselves

Make art not war

Despite years of war and destruction in Yemen, artists continue to make their marks of resistance in the damaged public squares and in private spaces. **Laura Silvia Battaglia** reports from two major cities

47(04): 68/70 | DOI: 10.1177/0306422018819352

UNDER THE TRADITIONAL arched loggias of one of the oldest streets in Aden, young Yemeni men challenge each other in endless games of five-a-side football. The guard, dressed in a shirt, *ma'wazz* (a skirt traditionally worn by Yemeni men) and slippers, and carrying a Kalashnikov, keeps them safe while he also collects tickets. The show is about to start and it's a sell-out. That's because tonight, like every night for the past three months, the hall will host a wedding.

It will be the 158th private screening of Ten Days before the Wedding, a comedy symbolising the rebirth of the city of Aden after the civil war. While hundreds still flock to the silver screen, such pleasure must remain private, as public screenings were banned in the 1990s and theatres across the country have all been shut down, damaged or destroyed.

Amr Gamal is not just the film's director, he is also a young defender of culture in the city of Aden – a catalyst of enthusiasm and cultural activism. He said: "This film is not our creation, it is the joint work of the people of Aden. It is the first all-Yemeni film ever made because everyone – the director, the actors, the extras, the producers – comes from Yemen. No one lives abroad, no one is foreign. This film is the city's natural reaction to war and it is the best and most peaceful response Aden could have."

Ten Days Before the Wedding is the final link in a chain of actions and reactions that young people have made into a permanent fixture of local life – from art and photography exhibitions to the demonstrations held two years ago when militias invaded the city and four nuns from the Missionaries of Charity were murdered.

Some members of the audience cry as the story reaches its most tragic point: when a number of obstacles nearly derail the marriage between Rasha and Mamoun, whose life has been thrown into turmoil by the 2015 conflict.

Art in Yemen is the only way to express peaceful resistance to war because all militias tend to cancel, silence and persecute any form of free expression.

Gamal and his team revel in the scene that plays out night after night while also planning an international roll out – they hope at the Berlin film festival.

For many years, Sarah Abdulrashid has been working to revive and bring culture to all corners of the city. The young Yemeni woman has spearheaded so many events that she now has a role in parliament.

"I was able to take exhibitions, cultural events, and book fairs from the city's streets to government, involving 12 national politicians in the process," she said. "Our aim is to make it easier for young people to engage with art and for artists in civil society to engage with politics. That's why we are trying to spotlight the oldest quarter of our city, because of its links to our traditions and shared history."

The Crater district of Aden is a prime example. Activists have made this neighbourhood of houses in the bowl of an extinct volcano the focus of their efforts for some time now. "Crater is a distillation of the country's past and present," Gamal explains. "In a few square metres it has the Crater Hotel, which was occupied by Houthi militias on their arrival in the city and

Civil society in Sana'a has not died, it has fallen silent

later became a symbol of the war when it was wracked by bombs and fire; across from the hotel is a mosque representing our indigenous tradition; while facing it is a vestige of the British Protectorate – the stadium. Along the street from this is the home of poet Arthur Rimbaud."

As he points to it, Gamal's eyes shine and the corners of his mouth turn down in a mixture of emotion and anger. "Almost no one knows it's there and no one cares about it. In a different country, this building would have been celebrated as a monument whereas here it's a private home to families living in poverty, falling to pieces around them."

While one city is being brought back to life, another struggles on. Sana'a, formerly the capital of Yemen and now centre of the Houthi occupation government, experienced a period of artistic ferment after the 2011 uprising.

Street artist Murad Subay still lives in Sana'a. His depictions of martyrs from the 2011 revolution fill the city's walls, especially in the Hadda district, in an attempt to champion a future free of dictatorship. His work is overshadowed by emblems of the Ansarullah Houthi party, but he remains defiant.

"Art gives me strength and gives strength to [other] people, so I do not leave the

ABOVE AND NEXT PAGE: Murad Subay's street art in San'aa, Yemen

Street art is a weapon that hits without killing and, on the contrary, gives hope to people

→ country," he said. "This is the way I know to fight: street art is a weapon that hits without killing and, on the contrary, gives hope to people. During the revolution in 2011 I thought I had seen the worst, but no: it was nothing compared to the war that broke out three years ago, and that continues today."

And there are others who refuse to give up. Mohammed al Shaidani is one of them, a street artist and friend of Subay. He was part of the 2014 campaign in which Subay asked citizens to join him in painting the city's walls, an initiative which not only taught those involved how to use spray paint but also made them the voice of civil society.

Al Shaidani set up a social campaign of his own, similar to the BookCrossing initiative. "It's called Open Book and is an ongoing means of promoting a culture of reading which doesn't have to be about religion or education. People do not read a lot in Yemen," he said. "We started this project in 2014 and are keeping it going. The books are not left on benches or in specific spots around the city to be passed from reader to reader, but [are] exchanged at small events held in coffee shops or private homes. Back in

the beginning, we used to do it in the street."

The main reason for this relocation was safety. The militias don't like the activists, most of whom are young supporters of the Muslim Brotherhood-affiliated Islah party or have closer ties to the secular world.

Mohammed al Dahri is a journalist, originally from Sadah, in northern Yemen, where the Houthi rebels have their stronghold. He shares nothing of their ideology. Also a friend of Subay, he took part in the street art campaign with his daughters, one aged 10, the other aged five. Both were eager to show photos of themselves standing by a wall holding spray cans.

He said: "Civil society in Sana'a has not died, it has fallen silent. In recent years, we used our voice to call for freedom and for equality between the disproportionate numbers of rich and poor, but we were silenced by the absence of law. No one in Yemen has any respect for the law and citizens have no law or constitution to appeal to. Both north and south are the realms of militias, subject to the rule of the most powerful, the kingdom of individuals."

He says many journalists have been arrested for not having written authorisation to hold a conference rather than for something critical they might have said. He sees the current period of transition as a lesson – a hard one – in civilisation.

"Outside intervention in this war has been catastrophic as it has made everything more difficult. Nevertheless, the conflict has taught us one thing – that Yemen belongs to all 30 million Yemeni, not to a group of one million with a particular viewpoint. We have to learn to live together and we have to do it quickly, for the future." ⊗

*Translation by **Denise Muir***

***Laura Silvia Battaglia** is the Index contributing editor for Yemen and Iraq. She has just returned from Yemen*

Truth or dare

Nobel Prize-winning author **Svetlana Alexievich**, who rarely gives interviews, talks to **Sally Gimson** about why she became a writer, and how she carries on, despite the threats

47(04): 71/72 | DOI: 10.1177/0306422018819353

SVETLANA ALEXIEVICH SAYS she is not scared. What will be will be.

"As a writer living in a post-Soviet space, I have got used to the fact that writers are always under threat. It's part of everyday life," the author from Belarus told Index ahead of being presented with the Anna Politkovskaya award in March.

The global award honours the memory of the journalist, writer and human rights activist who was shot dead because of her reporting about the war in Chechnya. Since Politkovskaya's death in 2006, life has got more dangerous for journalists and writers in the post-Soviet world.

It is normal, believes Alexievich, to be in conflict with the powers that be. "What is much more complicated and tragic is to be in conflict with your own people," she said.

Index caught up with her in Bratislava, where she was talking to the Central European Forum about her work.

Alexievich, who was born in 1948 – the daughter of a village schoolteacher who was buried with his communist party card – is celebrated through the world for her moving and

---

Life was very mysterious, terrible and fascinating and books were flat, patriotic and boring

remarkable books about the experiences and memories of ordinary people caught up in some of the most significant events of modern history.

In The Unwomanly Face of War she talks to women who were sent to the front in World War II. In her other books she explores the aftermath of the nuclear disaster in Chernobyl, the war in Afghanistan and, in Second-hand Time, the collapse of the Soviet Union.

But recently Alexievich, who lived for several years of her life in self imposed exile, but is now living in Minsk, has found that she is out of sync with the very people whose experiences she has written about. And that is worrying for her.

"So in Belarus, 80% supposedly are for [President Alexander] Lukashenko. In Russia, 70% are for [President Vladimir] Putin, and that's very, very difficult. There's no way out. You just have to do your job. It's unpleasant, but I am not scared.

"When I am in Russia, I am accused of being a Russophobe and a Banderite [a Ukrainian nationalist]. I come to Ukraine and I am accused of all sorts of things by this website." The Ukrainian nationalist website Myrotvorets has said she is anti-Ukrainian, and she was forced to cancel an appearance in Odessa because of threats against her.

How does she feel about all this? "We are all fatalists," she said. "Writers used to live in these conditions and, besides, I am 70 years old and at that age you can take these things with a pinch of salt and calmly."

Alexievich goes on to talk about her friend, the Belarusian-born journalist Pavel Grigorievich Sheremet, who was assassinated in a car bombing in 2016 in Kiev.

"I saw him a few months earlier, and he talked about love and how he loves Ukraine and he said he would talk to me more about love the next time I saw him," she said. He never did.

Alexievich has spent her life writing about ordinary people's experiences. "My own president, Lukashenko, says I am slandering both the Russian and the Belarus nations. He →

This is the question I grappled with the whole time I was writing the books. Why doesn't suffering make you free?

→ claims my books are slanderous because they cast aspersions on the country's great past, although I find it hard to understand how you fit gulag into that great past."

Her books are a challenge because "there is an official truth and the governments are trying to appropriate the collective memory".

She says Putin wants people to remember the great victory of World War II and the glories of the Soviet empire which followed. And that official version of the truth is gaining ground.

BELOW: Author and Nobel prize winner Svetlana Alexievich in 2016 at the launch of her book Chernobyl Prayer in Ukraine

Alexievich has fallen out with many friends who support the annexation of Crimea by the Russians, and this is a source of great sadness. "It is very difficult when I go to Russia and I don't know whether they approve of the annexation of Crimea or not. In this respect, many people took Putin's side."

She found it hurtful when some of the mothers of the soldiers who died in Afghanistan sued her for libel over her book Boys in Zinc - the zinc referring to the coffins they were brought home in. She says they had been encouraged by the generals, but there was something deeper.

"What was really shocking was the story of this woman who really wanted to tell the story of her son," she said. "She had this only son. He was drafted to Afghanistan and he shouldn't have been. They shouldn't have taken only sons, but clearly someone else had bribed someone so their son didn't have to go.

"When he was killed, when the coffin came back, she looked at it with these crazed eyes, and she threw herself on the coffin. And she started knocking on the coffin [saying]: 'Is it you my son? It is such a small coffin and you were two metres tall.' And then I saw her in the courtroom. She had wanted me to write her story, and she was testifying against me. I said: 'I wrote it exactly how you told me… and now you are here'. And she said: 'I need my son to be a hero'."

Alexievich added: "It's very, very difficult. Even such powerful suffering doesn't liberate you. This is the question I grappled with the whole time I was writing the books. Why doesn't suffering make you free?"

Her motivation for doing difficult, truthful writing comes from her childhood, where she lived in a house surrounded by books, but "none of them told the truth". "Suddenly the stories I heard from real life were very different," she said. "Life was very mysterious, terrible and fascinating and books were flat, patriotic and boring." ⊗

Sally Gimson is deputy editor at Index on Censorship

CREDIT: Roman Pilipey/EPA/Rex/Shutterstock

From armed rebellion to radical radio

Just ahead of the 25th anniversary of the Zapatista uprising in Mexico, **Stephen Woodma**n reports on how their movement has changed and now runs its own radio station and schools

47(04): 73/75 I DOI: 10.1177/0306422018819354

HIGH IN THE foggy mountains of Mexico's southernmost state of Chiapas, a cluster of indigenous villages has rejected state services and interference. This is territory run by the Zapatistas, members of a group that stole the international spotlight when it seized power in the region on New Year's Day 1994.

The group is widely defined as libertarian-socialist. It has declared war against the Mexican state and believes in civil resistance.

As the 25th anniversary of the Zapatista uprising approaches, analysts agree the movement has drawn media attention to issues such as poverty and land rights. The massive social project has also had a lasting impact on freedom of expression for minorities in Chiapas.

Indigenous people in Zapatista communities take part in local councils with rotating membership so everyone has a direct say in decisions. Children in the territory attend autonomous schools. They learn indigenous rights and history, both topics which are almost absent from state curriculums.

Less widely known is Radio Insurgente, the official Zapatista station which broadcasts across the territory from secret locations. Funded largely by donations, the clandestine channel offers a mix of local news, music and politics. The station says it aims to serve as "the voice of the voiceless".

Jorge Santiago, a former development worker based in Chiapas, told Index that the Zapatistas have energised independent media in the state.

"For many years, there was little concrete knowledge about life in the indigenous communities because no media outlets were close to them," said Santiago, who was detained as a suspected Zapatista leader in 1995 but released after two months because of a lack of evidence.

"Since the rebellion, many organisations have emerged to fill this void," he added. "This alternative media has shaped thinking within the communities and generated reflection outside them."

Alongside community groups such as Radio Insurgente, independent collectives including Promedios and Koman Ilel have raised awareness of the challenges facing indigenous groups.

While the armed Zapatista uprising lasted only 12 days, Santiago says the rebellion provided the group with an international platform that they continue to exploit to this day.

Subcomandante Marcos, real name Rafael Sebastián Guillén Vicente, is the balaclava-clad former Zapatista spokesman, who has helped generate public interest and sympathy for the movement. Although he officially retired in 2014, market vendors in Chiapas still offer handcrafted Marcos dolls as souvenirs, and T-shirts and badges bearing his masked image are popular throughout the state.

The rebels continue to bypass the mostly negative coverage on national television and radio. They have always maintained a distance from foreign Marxist movements. Instead, they locate their struggle within the context of the 500-year mistreatment of Mexico's indigenous population. →

The station says it aims to serve as 'the voice of the voiceless'

Many journalists say the Zapatista project has had a lasting impact on their work. Alejandro Páez, then aged 25, travelled to Chiapas in 1994 as a correspondent for El Diario de Juárez newspaper.

"[The rebellion] gave me a deeper understanding of Mexico," Páez said. "It forced me to read about extreme poverty and what it means to be abandoned... In fact, the events forced the whole country to face its indigenous groups, its poor."

The Zapatistas failed in their original aim of sparking an armed revolution in 1994. As a result, they began to talk less about violent struggle and focused on social projects such as setting up alternative governments in Chiapas.

Today, the movement runs autonomous communities across five regions of the state, with a population of around 300,000.

Zapatista leaders play a key role in planning and decision-making. But for local matters, a democratic system is in place, with residents taking turns to sit on local councils.

"The Zapatista democracy encourages indigenous people to take part in the political process," said Adela Cedillo, a PhD student at the University of Wisconsin-Madison who has studied the movement in Chiapas. "People

BELOW: Children sit in a local schoolhouse of a Zapatista community in Chiapas, Mexico

CREDIT: Giles Clarke/Getty

discuss issues related to their daily lives, such as crop management and community work."

The rebels also run their own education system in the autonomous territories. These centres are very different from public schools, where Spanish is the classroom language and the curriculum imposes outside norms and values on indigenous children.

Many of the autonomous schools are bilingual, so students preserve fluency in an indigenous language. The Zapatista curriculum also celebrates local knowledge and customs.

"There is a genuine interest in connecting students with their roots and histories," Cedillo said. "These schools are doing their best to initiate a cultural revival."

But the prospect of violence looms over daily life in the region. In 2014, paramilitaries attacked the Zapatistas at a dialogue between rebels and local farmers. The assailants killed a Zapatista schoolteacher and wounded 15 others.

For many, the violence brought back memories of the 1997 massacre in the village of Acteal. In that attack, government loyalists stormed a church and murdered 45 people – mostly women and children – because they supported the Zapatistas.

While these bloody incidents caused a stir across Mexico, the press has mostly ignored the movement since the 1994 rebellion. The reduced media interest has restricted the group's ability to exert national influence.

The rebels put forward María de Jesús Patricio Martínez as a candidate for Mexico's presidential election this year. She made history as the first indigenous woman to run for president in the country. As an independent candidate, she needed to collect more than 850,000 signatures from registered voters to earn a place on the ballot. However, she was disqualified from the race after her campaigners managed to collect fewer than 250,000.

Meanwhile, Zapatistas have formed links with international activists online.

They were one of the first radical groups to understand the importance of the internet. That online strategy became a model for later movements

"The Zapatistas have not limited themselves to local struggles," said Isain Mandujano, the Chiapas correspondent for Proceso magazine. "They were one of the first radical groups to understand the importance of the internet. That online strategy became a model for later movements."

In fact, they have tended to have greater impact beyond Mexico's borders in recent years.

"Indigenous movements in Latin America study their strategies," said Leonidas Oikonomakis, an academic at the University of Crete who has researched the Zapatistas. "They almost always seek autonomy."

By pursuing freedom from the state's institutions, these groups hope to set their own agenda on education and information.

Zapatista principles also resonate in European countries such as Greece and Spain, where governments have sought to restrict the right to protest. Many activist groups in these countries have adopted the kind of participatory democracy they would like to see extend into wider society.

"In Greece and Spain, social movements rotate positions of power and are always talking about the Zapatistas," Oikonomakis said.

He adds that the movement offers hope to any group that feels ignored by mainstream politics.

"I have seen Zapatista influences all over the globe," Oikonomakis said. "They offer a proposal that resonates everywhere." ⊗

Stephen Woodman _is contributing editor, Mexico, for Index on Censorship. He is based in Guadalajara_

PICTURED: A boy covers his ears in a refugee camp, Syria.

CULTURE

78 DANGEROUS CHOICES <u>LIWAA YAZJI</u>
The Syrian playwright speaks to **Lewis
Jennings** about self-censorship and how this
has influenced her exclusive new play

88 SWEAT THE SMALL STUFF <u>NEEMA KOMBA</u>
Rachael Jolley introduces a short story from
the award-winning Tanzanian writer Neema
Komba, who talks weddings, cake and the
censorship of bloggers

94 POWER PLAY <u>YURI HERRERA</u>
The acclaimed Mexican author reveals how
geopolitical borders are influencing his work.
We also publish a newly translated short story

Dangerous choices

Syrian playwright **Liwaa Yazji's** new play deals with a mother's choice when her writing puts her and her family in danger. **Lewis Jennings** talks to her

47(04): 78/87 I DOI: 10.1177/0306422018819355

LEFT: Syrian playwright Liwaa Yazji. Her play Goats was performed at The Royal Court Theatre in London in 2017

WHEN WHAT YOU write can result in torture and death for you or your loved ones, it can be difficult to express how you are feeling. But Syrian playwright Liwaa Yazji refuses to let this hinder her work.

"If I decide to stop writing then the enemy – or the dictatorship, shall we say – succeeds in making me shut up, whether I am inside or outside the country," she said. "So it's kind of dealing with your own censorship and fears."

Yazji studied English literature at Damascus University and started her writing career in Syria before moving to Berlin. Her play, Goats, was performed at London's Royal Court Theatre in 2017.

Her new play addresses the bleak consequences of avoiding self-censorship and is based on what is happening to people she knows in Syria.

"I will not exaggerate and say I am scared to be killed because of my work, but I am scared because I still have family there and I could be detained or imprisoned there. Sometimes I like to close my eyes and think this is not going to happen, but I must also calculate the danger," said Yazji.

"It is always a question of how to speak my mind, my opinion, and how to be true to what I believe and still not put myself in the situation where my family are affected over there. It's about selflessness and selfishness."

Her new play, Waiting for the Guests, written exclusively for Index and published for the first time below, looks at what happens when a mother's writing makes her an enemy of the state and she is forced to make the crushing decision either to wait and be killed by soldiers, or to kill herself and her family before the soldiers get to them.

Yazji said: "The horror of waiting at home for someone to come and kill you, but then deciding 'no, I don't want to be killed by them, I will do it first'. That whole situation, the fear and horror, the moment when you decide, it stays with me. I put myself in that situation and how I would fictionalise and dramatise that."

What is happening in Syria has a great impact on her work, and she has previously told Index about the "big responsibility" she has when writing about what goes on in the country. Nonetheless, the playwright warns, the chaotic scenes in Syria could happen anywhere. "You're always in danger." ⊗

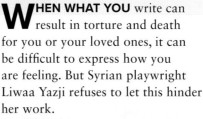

Sometimes I like to close my eyes and think this is not going to happen

Lewis Jennings is the editorial assistant at Index on Censorship

Waiting for the Guests

By **Liwaa Yazji**

Characters

MOTHER Mid-thirties

FATHER Mid-thirties

DAUGHTER Aged nine

SON Aged six

The events take place in a one-storey house with simple, modern decor in a city in Syria in 2014.

SCENE ONE

> *Kitchen. A window looks out on a balcony that is enclosed on all but one side. The door to the balcony is closed, as are the shutters on the door. The room is dimly lit. Mother opens the refrigerator, takes out all the items inside and places them on the kitchen counter. She opens the cupboards and takes out the few provisions that remain. She puts pasta on to boil. She opens the last bags of rice and bulgur and impassively pours them onto the floor.*
>
> *She inspects the flame under the pot of pasta. The flame is burning low – clearly the gas has almost run out.*
>
> *She turns back to the cupboard, takes out the appliances, including a stand mixer and fancy espresso machine, as well as a set of dishes. She piles the appliances next to the gas tank. She selects four plates and bowls and sets them aside. Then she begins throwing the rest of the dishes onto the floor, one by one, tranquilly observing how the broken shards scatter. She does the same thing with a set of cups that appear brand new: she sets aside four cups and then calmly throws the rest on the floor. She places the dishes and cups she reserved on the kitchen counter.*
>
> *The telephone rings offstage. It seems as though someone answers.*
>
> *Mother turns to the rest of the dishes and cups and throws them on the floor, all but the set of four she reserved. She does this slowly, watching each one break.*
>
> *Daughter enters the kitchen. Mother gestures at her not to come any closer. Daughter looks around in shock and incomprehension. She is about to ask something.*

MOTHER We agreed, no questions today.

→ *Daughter remains silent. She leaves.*

Mother finishes breaking everything. She turns to the balcony shutters and opens one side to look out. The sharp light of day enters the room all at once, preventing her from being able to see well. She closes the shutters.

She turns to the counter. She picks up a piece of potato; it is clearly old, and she tries to clean it. She switches on the tap, but no water comes out. She checks the pasta on the stove. She sits at the table and puts a potato and onion in front of her. She begins to chop the onion and starts to cry.

Father appears in the kitchen doorway and looks at her. He looks around the kitchen.

MOTHER Who was it?

FATHER Ammar.

MOTHER How long?

FATHER Two hours… maybe.

Mother nods.

MOTHER They're definitely coming?

Father nods in response.

FATHER How long do you need?

Mother looks at the clock.

SCENE TWO

Mother and Father's bedroom. The window is closed, but the shutters are slightly open, with broken light coming in between the slats. From offstage, the sound of cabinets being opened and closed. Daughter sits on the edge of the bed. In front of her are a set of coloured markers. Father enters. He is carrying a utility knife. Daughter watches him closely.

DAUGHTER What should I draw?

Father sits down next to her and starts slicing open the pillows, one by one. Feathers fly around. Daughter rushes to open the pillows and scatter the feathers. She seems happy, if anxious.

FATHER What do you like best about our house?

DAUGHTER The house.

> *She walks over to a blank wall. With a marker, she begins to make a small drawing of a house.*

FATHER *(While shredding the mattress)* Across all of it.

> *Daughter watches him for a moment. Then she makes a bigger drawing of the house, and*

→ *draws the interior of the house as well.*

DAUGHTER Who's coming over today? Mum won't say. Do we like them? Do they like us?

Sound of a shell landing somewhere not far away. Son enters, afraid. He sees the feathers flying around and Daughter drawing on the wall. He seems stunned.

SON Did you hear?

DAUGHTER It's been closer.

FATHER Have you finished what your mother asked?

SON I put my clothes next to yours on the floor. I'm scared.

Father turns to the mirror and smashes it with his fist. Daughter stops drawing. Offstage, the telephone rings.

SCENE THREE

Living room. Books line the shelves, and there is a flat screen TV. The room is filled with clothing piled on the floor, next to Son and Daughter's toys. The window shutters are closed; the room is lit with LED lights and a few battery-powered lamps. Son and Daughter are alone on the sofa. Daughter seems nervous. Son is busy looking around.

Silence.

DAUGHTER You feel it?

Son doesn't respond.

DAUGHTER I love you anyway.

Son remains silent.

DAUGHTER Tell me that you love me too!

SON Love you.

DAUGHTER Say it for real.

SON What do you mean?

Daughter hugs him.

DAUGHTER Come on, let's say it together, at the same time. One. Two. Three.

BOTH I love you.

Daughter lets go of Son. He stares at the piles of his toys. He is about to go towards them.

DAUGHTER Don't touch anything.

Son goes back to the sofa, giving in to boredom.

DAUGHTER Tell me something, was it you who scribbled on the picture above my bed? And did you scribble under my doll's eye?

SON No.

DAUGHTER It was me who threw your Playmobil out of the window. Were you the one who scribbled on her?

Son shakes his head in response, annoyed with her.

SON I don't wanna talk to you any more.

DAUGHTER It was me who left the birdcage open.

SON I know. But I didn't say anything.

Sounds of bombing.

SON It's louder today. A lot louder.

DAUGHTER Did you hide anything?

SON My dinosaur. Enough.

DAUGHTER I hid a notebook.

Daughter whispers in Son's ear. Then he whispers in her ear. They both smile. Silence. Daughter hugs Son again, tightly. Father enters.

SON Why did you shut the door? What were you and Mum doing?

FATHER What were *you* two doing?

Mother enters carrying the four dishes and crosses to put them down on the centre table. Father exits. Mother exits. Father returns with bread, cups and water. He exits. Mother returns with pasta. She exits. Father returns carrying a dish of tuna, and another dish with all the tinned food they have left. Mother returns with a coffee pot, a sugar jar and biscuits. Father observes the table, as does Mother, trying to determine what is missing. A moment of confusion.

SON Do we have to wait?

RIGHT: A woman walks through the rubble of Homs, Syria in 2013 before rebels and civilians finally withdraw from the city

→ *Mother sits down, then Father.*

MOTHER Is anything of yours left in there?

Son and Daughter shake their heads "no", looking at each other. Mother remembers something and rushes off. The telephone rings. Father gets up to answer it. Mother returns, stands nearby.

FATHER Yeah... and where were they? The co-operative building.

Mother gestures as if trying to figure out whether a nearby building is the one he is referring to. Father gestures in response. She quickly exits while he continues the conversation on the phone. She returns carrying a box filled with cassette tapes of old music and several notebooks that look like journals and diaries. She exits again. She returns with a cloth bag.

FATHER *(Engaged in conversation on the phone.)* Amal's house? Okay... and Salam? Too?! Azza? Abdullah? Who's left? Us? We're about to start dinner... and you lot? *(Father jerks his ear away from the phone as if he were shaken by a loud noise on the other end.)* . . . Hello... hello...

Father tries to listen a bit longer then hangs up, now clearly concerned. Daughter looks at him expectantly. Mother sits down next to Daughter and opens the cloth bag.

MOTHER Come here.

Father walks over to them and sits down. Mother gives Daughter several pieces of gold jewellery. Daughter takes them, not understanding.

MOTHER Put it on!

DAUGHTER They're ugly! You want them to see me wearing this when they—

MOTHER All of it.

Daughter puts the jewellery on, while mother puts the rest on herself. Mother puts a necklace around son's neck. Father watches. Mother takes two wedding rings from among the jewellery, and offers her ring to father. She is overcome with tears, as is he. She extends her hand, and he places the ring on her finger. She looks at him expectantly, and he extends his hand too. She puts his ring on his finger.

MOTHER Kiss me.

Father kisses Mother quickly.

MOTHER Kiss me for real.

Father is flustered, then kisses Mother. Sounds of shelling and an exchange of gunfire outside.

MOTHER Let's eat.

→   *They begin to eat.*

SON Why aren't the fridge and washing machine and microwave where they usually are?

DAUGHTER Everything's next to the gas tank.

SON We ate before our guests got here. Is that ok?

MOTHER *(to Father)* They're coming for sure?

FATHER For sure.

MOTHER What if they don't arrive?

FATHER We agreed they will.

MOTHER Maybe…

DAUGHTER They're going to come.

    Mother and Father turn to Daughter fearfully.

DAUGHTER I know who's coming. I know why you're doing all this. So they won't be able to take anything.

    Mother holds back her tears.

DAUGHTER Are they coming for us because you wrote against them?

MOTHER That's got nothing to do with this…

DAUGHTER It does too.

FATHER They're coming for everyone.

SON Who's "they"?

DAUGHTER If you hadn't written anything, would they still be coming?

MOTHER No. Don't think like that.

DAUGHTER Are you lying to me?

FATHER No.

MOTHER We would never do anything that might hurt you.

DAUGHTER But you're against them.

FATHER They're coming for everyone… they're not going to ask first.

MOTHER *(to Father)* Call Ammar!

Father hesitates. Then he stands and dials Ammar's number. No one answers.

DAUGHTER Uncle Ammar in the building across the street?

Mother hugs Daughter.

MOTHER *(to Father)* Call Um Salma.

He dials the next number. No one answers.

FATHER They must be in the building.

Daughter cries. Mother hugs her, struggling to keep Daughter and Son from seeing that she is overcome with tears. Father walks over to the sofa where they are sitting, reaches underneath and pulls out a grenade. Daughter is frightened. Mother hugs the children. Father, holding the grenade, joins them on the sofa. Mother looks at him anxiously.

MOTHER *(Fearfully)* Well?

Father thinks, then hands the grenade to Son.

MOTHER No.

FATHER *(to Son)* Hold it like this, son. . . and pull here. (Indicating the firing pin.)

Son is scared of Mother's and Daughter's reactions.

DAUGHTER No. . .

SON I don't wanna.

FATHER There's no time. For my sake… for all our sakes… if you love us, if you don't want anyone to hurt us.

Son pulls the firing pin.

Explosion.

....

Translated by **Elisabeth Jaquette**
....

Liwaa Yazji *is a Syrian playwright, whose work has been performed at London's Royal Court*

Sweat the small stuff

Tanzanian flash fiction writer and poet **Neema Komba** talks cake, weddings and being silenced with **Rachael Jolley**

47(04): 88/93 I DOI: 10.1177/0306422018819356

"**H**OW CAN YOU make it about small things that matter to you?" asks poet Neema Komba, describing the motivation for her new short story, published for the first time below.

Let Them Eat Fruit Cake is set in her native Tanzania and describes the challenge of a woman trying to stand up for her own wishes and feelings as others try to bulldoze over her while arranging her wedding via committee.

Wedding committees are normal in Tanzania, where a group of, often older, people will organise the day on the couple's behalf. Sometimes the bride-to-be is not even invited to join the committee, although things are starting to change.

Komba, 31, who is a 2014 Etisalat prize winner for flash fiction literature, said: "It was about trying to figure out how it doesn't just stop at the top level. People lose their voices at the smallest things."

People lose their voices at the smallest things

The inspiration for the story of the wedding cake came partly from her experience when her brother was married a few years ago and someone on the wedding committee attempted to stop the family getting the wedding they wanted.

"We ended up alienating him and he was like the chair of the wedding committee but he didn't really end up doing anything and we took over," she said.

The family story speaks to a much wider situation in Tanzania at the moment, where bloggers are being forced offline by the need for a licence that costs as much as many annual incomes. Other new rules include fines or a jail sentence for publishing material that is "indecent", "annoying" or that "leads to public disorder", as well as mandatory surveillance cameras in cybercafes.

"A few years ago we had so much freedom we could pretty much say anything about the president. At the time we still thought he was a pretty awful person, but now we have a new one and now, in terms of freedom of speech, things are really terrible," said Komba.

As a writer, Komba feels strongly about what is going on around her and has been mulling over how to respond to it. Her story, she thinks, considers how if you don't address small issues, and speak up for what you believe in, they can boil over "and become something huge, because it is not being addressed".

With the story she tries to confront "how you could really lose your voice, even in a normal setting, because when you are looking at it from a family perspective you can think: 'What can I do, I am so small?'."

She added: "It was about trying to figure out how it doesn't just stop at the top level. People lose their voices at the smallest things."

The story is, she says, "a wake-up call even to myself. As a writer I've been really afraid to say things, because, well, if I say this I am tipping the scales a bit".

"I felt it was also to remind myself things become worse if you don't address them at the time," she added. "They can continue and get worse."

Komba, who has a business degree and runs a soap factory when she is not writing, is using her experiences in her next piece of writing, a memoir she has just finished. Her other ambition is to write a book about important women who have made a difference in Tanzania. ⊗

Rachael Jolley is editor of Index on Censorship

Let them eat fruit cake

ON A BREEZY August afternoon, the first mango flowers fell from the tree outside the Udasa club like pale yellow flurries. Tumaini clicked her heels against the gravel pavement outside the club. She could see the committee seated on a row of red plastic chairs under the neem tree beside a swing set where children played. She adjusted the *khanga* draped on her shoulder and lifted her right foot to take the first step towards the committee for her and Tito's wedding. Why was it so difficult to tell the *kamati* – her wedding committee – what she wanted?

"I want a vanilla cake." She practised the words in her mind. Simple. Definitive. She wasn't going to beg. After all, it was her wedding.

It was the third committee meeting, the day to pass the budget for the wedding, but it looked to be more of a get together to eat and drink. All afternoon, the *kamati* members sat in their chairs, eating *mishkaki* – roasted beef skewers – with chips and plantains, while slowly nursing their beers. There was no discussion about the wedding. Everything the chairman proposed was unanimously passed.

The *kamati* members were from Tito's side of the family. It's the groom's family that prepares the wedding, and Tumaini's family would simply be invited to attend. The send-off is the bride's ceremony. For the send-off, the bride's family would prepare the ceremony and the groom's family would be invited. It's tradition. Family and friends usually contribute money to attend a wedding, giving them some kind of say in the wedding – like shareholders, maybe even tax payers. The wedding committee is accountable to the contributors and to the family. They have almost a fiduciary duty to act in the best interest of the wedding contributors, to give them the best return on their contribution in the form of a lavish party with bottomless drinks, amazing food and entertainment. Some committees don't even care about the bride and groom, for whom the entire wedding committee is set.

This *kamati* was different. On the second meeting, they had invited Tumaini to be a part of the preparations. It was unheard of for a *kamati* to consider the bride's opinion and Tumaini was honoured that they cared for hers. She felt lucky that she could have the option to fulfil her wishes, but she wasn't particularly trying to overstep her boundaries. Tito worked at a gold mine and was often out of town, leaving Tumaini on her own.

She had never been one of those girls who dreamt of her wedding day in great detail – from the kind of flowers at the doorstep to the colour of her nail polish. She had been too busy caring for her four-month-old daughter, Kajala, to think about such details, but in that second meeting she felt like she owed it to them to give her opinion since they had gone out of their way to include her. So, when the chairman opened the floor for contributions, she wanted to give one.

"Is there anyone who has objections about the cake?" He smiled at the members, expecting total agreement from everyone. His eyes bulged when Tumaini raised her hand.

"*Mkwe* (in law), we haven't even married you yet and you are already trying to call the

→

shots?" He sneered at her and the other members laughed. Tumaini was confused. Didn't they say they wanted her opinion? Why invite her if they didn't mean it? She had tried again a few times in that meeting to get a word in, but the chair never let her speak.

"You are marrying into our tribe now," he told her. "Our women are reserved. *Sio kimbelembele* (not assertive)." Tumaini was offended by his remarks but didn't want to stir the pot, so she smiled.

The *mwenyekiti* (chairman), Mzee Kapalila, was Tito's uncle on his mother's side. He was a short and stout man, with erect shoulders that elevated his stature. He was a man of few words with a thick northern accent that made every sentence sound like a command. He didn't have any apparent charm, but people still took to him. He was on their side, promising the best use for their money. In tough economic times, people wanted that kind of assurance, someone that would use their money frugally. It didn't matter when he dictated how much the wedding dress should cost, or that his cousin should supply the drinks. According to Kapalila, it was better for the *kamati* to deal with someone he knew and trusted. So, when he proposed that his wife be the treasurer for the committee, everyone agreed without any hesitation.

Tito's mother had been grateful for Kapalila's involvement since Tito's father had passed away.

But the voice grew inside her stomach. It was a tornado, maybe a volcano. It seethed

---

She also thought she could enjoy her son's wedding without the stress of planning it. She could focus on getting her women's group to organise a bag party to give him presents to start his life. The wedding was just too big a production for her.

However, as *mwenyekiti*, Kapalila hated to be contradicted. The only opinion he wanted to hear was the one that agreed with his own.

After the second meeting, Kapalila pulled Tumaini aside.

"Listen, we are all here working to make your wedding great. Why are you making it so difficult?"

"I just …" Tumaini tried to explain, but he cut her off.

"These people are paying a great deal of money – they want to eat, they want to drink. Not all this other female nonsense – dress, decorations, cake!" He paused for a moment, then raised his voice to reach nearby committee members continuing to drink after the meeting was over.

"People want BEER!" The remaining *kamati* cheered.

Tumaini walked away unsure of what to do. It was her wedding, but was it really hers if someone else was paying for it? As she approached the blue metal gate, one of the *kamati* members, Mama Anasi, Tito's eldest cousin, ran after her.

CREDIT: Alex Green

→ "Baba means well," she said in a breathy voice. "We all just agree with him because we know he wants the best for the wedding." She said. "I know he can be a bit... much... sometimes, but he really cares." She placed her hand on Tumaini's shoulder to give her a bit of assurance. "You don't want to oppose him!" She flashed a big smile.

Maybe he really did care. Maybe he really meant well. He had pledged the most money for the wedding. He had yet to pay it, but he wanted to give two million shillings. Tumaini thought about it all the way home and decided to stay quiet about the cake. She wanted peace with the new family, peace on her wedding day. Silence was the best way to accomplish that – because it's simpler, she thought. All she had to do was stuff her voice in the deepest parts of herself, and to be their idea of a dutiful wife until the wedding passed.

* * *

THE MORNING BEFORE the third meeting, Tumaini woke up ready to accept everything for the wedding. She nursed Kajala and got ready for the meeting. She brushed her teeth and twisted her hair into neat knots. She draped a red *khanga* on her shoulder to give some colour to her black outfit. She dropped Kajala off at her mum's house.

She found her mother watching the news – about some banned hip-hop song that spoke ill of the government. Tumaini didn't pay attention to that kind of news and was surprised that her mother paid any mind to it.

"Silence is cancerous, it rots things," her mother said mindlessly before switching off the TV. "Someone somewhere has got to be brave for all of us."

"Silence is cancerous, it rots things," her mother said mindlessly before switching off the TV. "Someone somewhere has got to be brave for all of us"

It must have been her mother's words that became the catalyst to her thoughts all the way to the meeting. Suddenly she had this need to speak out at the committee.

She thought of how dishonest and shameful it was to feign apathy when she cared about the kind of cake they served at her wedding. How cowardly it was to choose silence. She thought about how embarrassed she had been to bring Kajala to the meeting – how she didn't want Kajala to see her mother so voiceless.

And so, that afternoon she found herself pacing outside the Udasa club searching for words to go against *mwenyekiti*. A trickle of sweat ran down her armpits and she could feel her blouse dampen. She took a step, then two, until she was face to face with the committee, but then she froze in their presence.

This wasn't just some committee. This was her future family. *Mwenyekiti* wasn't some tyrant. He was Tito's uncle, a man who had stepped into Tito's father's shoes to plan a wedding for them. Her words had consequences. Speaking could cost her the entire wedding, and even the love of her life. No vanilla cake could ever be that important. So, she pulled up a chair and sat silently at the edge of the group.

The treasurer was passing the budget. Everyone was mindlessly nodding to everything she said –

Speaking could cost her the entire wedding, and even the love of her life. No vanilla cake could ever be that important

---

like a bad catchy song – "*Ndio*. Yes. Of course."

"*Mkwe*!" Kapalila called to her. "*Karibu* (welcome)! You are just in time. We were discussing about how mama Kapalila here will make your wedding cake. She makes delicious fruit cakes."

There were more nods from the *kamati*.

"It costs next to nothing. Just one million." He gave her a sinister smile, then yelled at the waiter.

"Leta (bring) BEER!" He laughed, and just like that, the discussion was over. He ignored Tumaini again as if she were a decorative fixture with nothing to say.

Tumaini wanted peace. She clenched her fists and swallowed her voice deep inside her. But the voice grew inside her stomach. It was a tornado, maybe a volcano. It seethed. Like a reflux, it rose back to her chest all the way up to the tip of her tongue. She didn't mean to raise her voice, but the words came out louder and angrier than she intended.

"I don't want a fucking fruit cake! I want a vanilla cake – plain and simple. Is-It-Too-Much-To-Fucking-Ask?"

And the committee went silent.

....

Neema Komba *is an award-winning poet, author and journalist from Tanzania*

Power play

The conflict on the Mexican/US border is the setting for **Yuri Herrera's** fiction. **Jemimah Steinfeld** talks to the acclaimed author

47(04): 94/97 I DOI: 10.1177/0306422018819358

LEFT: Award-winning Mexican writer Yuri Herrera

UNLIKE THE PEOPLE who form the core of Yuri Herrera's novels – the dispossessed of Mexico's borderlands – Herrera does not face censorship in an obvious day-to-day way, a fact he is aware of and for which he is grateful.

"I am in a privileged place in terms of my work, a university, and I am equally privileged in that sense when I am in Mexico, because I have certain visibility and I work closely with certain institutions," he told Index.

Born in Actopan, Mexico, and having studied in both Mexico and the USA, Herrera is one of the most highly regarded authors to come out of Latin America today. His novel, Kingdom Cons, won the 2003 Premio Binacional de Novela/ Border of Words. Then Signs Preceding the End of the World became an instant global hit and was translated widely. Herrera is famous for using neologisms, invented words which often combine meanings. For instance, in the short story below the word "interruficated" expresses both the idea of interrupting and of suffocating.

Having lived in two countries, and having spent time in the border areas of El Paso and Ciudad Juárez, Herrera's writing centres predominantly on the experience of those living along the border between Mexico and the United States.

"Geopolitical borders have been part of the models I use in order to develop my stories, but I also try to speak about what I call "the border condition", which defines spaces in which, even though they might be far away from the geopolitical borders, you find different communities exchanging values, habits, goods, sometimes clashing, but that function as a laboratory for new identities, political practices, linguistic forms.

"Now, in these spaces, we have also seen a replication of the worst part of the border spaces: institutions and individuals persecuting undocumented workers, harassing people just because they look or sound different," he said.

Today, Herrera teaches at the University of Tulane in New Orleans. While his current home might not provide quite the censored environment of Mexico, a nation sliding down free speech indexes at breakneck speed, Herrera is keen to point out that this does not make it immune.

"There are different ways of censorship, not only government censorship or the threats from organised crime (that is, when it is a different thing, because very often they are one and the same, in either country), but also there is the censorship practised by the big corporations that own newspapers and publishing houses. That happens quite frequently in the United States, even though it is not discussed openly very often."

The short story below was originally published in Talud, a Spanish volume of short stories, and has been translated into English for the first time for Index. It considers how the those in power intimidate others and shut them down.

"It is about the supposed rationality of the powerful, how we are duped by their aura of knowledge when, in fact, many times they make decisions based on their personal ambitions and how they justify themselves with certain superstitions (sometimes disguised as economic theories, for example)," said Herrera. ⊗

Jemimah Steinfeld is a deputy editor for Index on Censorship

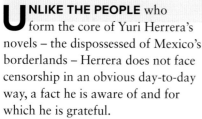

It is about the supposed rationality of the powerful, how we are duped by their aura of knowledge

Omens

THE PRESIDENT LOOKED at his imbecile serving as co-ordinator of advisers and said:

"Bring me a chicken."

The addressee, who'd been in the process of enumerating for his boss the benefits that the experts had laid out for him of selling the refineries to the Chinese and not the gringos, interrufficated himself as if to say, Wha…?

"A chicken – alive," the president confirmed, "and a frog, and a *tlacuache*. We'll settle this here and now."

He stared fixedly at the co-ordinator of advisers, who realised the order was, in fact, serious and set off in search of the animals.

Why had he asked for a *tlacuache*? the president wondered. He didn't even really know what a *tlacuache* looked like – essentially an opossum, he thought. He'd seen a documentary at one point but couldn't recall the animal's appearance. Regardless, its name had a resonance that would serve to better illustrate his point. He ordered the smaller swimming pool to be emptied and the co-ordinator of advisers to meet him there with the animals. On arriving, he saw that the hen was fat and white, that the frog was wet and had bumpy skin – so much so that he wondered if it were, perhaps, a toad but didn't dare to ask – and that the *tlacuache* resembled a sort of ill-tempered beaver. He nodded in approval.

"Set them loose, and observe," the president ordered. The co-ordinator of advisers opened the little cages in which he was carrying the animals.

There was a moment of bewildered tranquility in the pool, as though the animals were attempting to make sense of the extraordinary confluence of circumstances that had them now contemplating one another, these different species; then the chicken pounced on the frog, which hopped up toward the edge of the pool without completely clearing it. The amphibian then rolled dramatically to the bottom of the pool and would have been pecked to death were it not for the *tlacuache*, which at that moment lunged ferociously at the hen, attacking with claws and teeth. The frog made another unfruitful attempt to depart from the pool and then remained very still as the chicken flapped ceaselessly against the *tlacuache*'s onslaught. This persecution lasted a good three minutes, until the frog committed the tactical error of seeking a safer refuge and had just taken one discreet little hop when the *tlacuache*, enflamed by battle, landed on the amphibian, eviscerating it in a matter of seconds. The hen continued flailing in the air a bit longer and then stopped, though prey to great agitation. Her clucking and the mammal's soft chewing were all that could be heard for a time; then the *tlacuache* turned and attacked the bird once more.

"Enough," said the head of state. "Separate them."

The co-ordinator of advisers was forced to climb down into the pool and kick the marsupial in order to save the bird.

"So," the president said. "How do we interpret this?"

The co-ordinator of advisers glanced at him in a mix of panic and despair. Suddenly aware of what he must look like, he let go of the over-excited hen so that it could run free, and searched for words.

"Well, well, well," he turned to look at the *tlacuache* in the pool, possibly attempting to determine whether it had been the triumphant animal. "The…the lesson is…that the best prey is not the juiciest, but the safest bet…and…and…that he who puts up the most fight must be shown who's really in charge…all the time."

The co-ordinator of advisers closed his mouth and anxiously awaited his Lord's reply.

"So that's the lesson, is it?" the president asked derisively. "No, amigo, the lesson is that I must choose as my right hand someone who thinks for himself, not someone who falls for anything. Be off. And set that animal free."

That night he thought maybe he should send the co-ordinator of advisers to the Vatican as an attaché. Let the man callus his fingers on rosary beads. But just before going to sleep he was given a memorandum: the Chinese had made an offer matching the conditions set by the gringos, who – having found out about the deal who knows how – made it known that they had faith in the government's word and were prepared to add some individual compensation, provided they were the beneficiaries of the deal. Mmm. Suddenly he had both delegations where he wanted them. The president couldn't help but think of the calm way the frog had placed itself within reach of the *tlacuache* while the latter pounced on the bigger prey. There had been a touch of resignation, the president noted; he thought the frog's final hop had signified an acceptance of its fate. In truth, the battle with the bird had only left the frog in a more vulnerable position. Like with the gringos.

Son of a bitch, thought the president, now he really did have to fire the imbecile co-ordinator of advisers. He put on a flannel robe and went to his office to reflect. Through the picture window he watched a cat inch patiently closer to a rat that was devouring scraps in the residence gardens. Just as the cat was about to trap it, the rodent escaped. The president hadn't known that there were either cats or rats in the gardens, he'd have to inquire about this.

"Jesus," he sighed, "governing is so damn hard."

....

Translated by **Lisa Dillman**

....

Yuri Herrera *is a bestselling Mexican writer currently based in the USA. His first novel, Trabajos del reino, won the 2003 Premio Binacional de Novela/Border of Words and made Herrera one of the most famous writers in Latin America*

INDEX AROUND THE WORLD

Artists fight on against censors

It's been 50 years since plays were signed off by the Lord Chamberlain in the UK, but artists are still under attack throughout the world, writes **Lewis Jennings**

47(04): 98/100 | DOI: 10.1177/0306422018819359

"**IT HAD TO** go through a rigorous censorship machine via the Lord Chamberlain and there were some things taken out and changed, things that by today's standards would be completely fine and would go ahead," said Index magazine deputy editor Jemimah Steinfeld about The Vortex, a once-controversial play by Noël Coward written in the 1920s.

"It shows just how arbitrary censorship is. What we think is offensive today is not what someone else will think is offensive tomorrow," Steinfeld added.

"That's just one reason why we should safeguard and promote artists' rights to cause offence, and why we need to be vigilant about censorship which still happens today in the arts, both in the UK and abroad."

Steinfeld was speaking after hosting a Coward-funded theatre and censorship workshop at the British Library in London. The Index event featured live performances from actors and audience members and coincided with the 50th anniversary of the 1968 Theatres Act, which abolished censorship in playhouses around Britain.

Coward's work became a regular target for the Lord Chamberlain's Office, a department within the British Royal Household, which had a pivotal role in censoring theatre performed in Britain prior to 1968. Theatre companies such as The Royal Court Theatre came into regular conflict with the committee.

Actor Matthew Romain, who performed a scene from The Vortex with fellow actor Jennifer Leong, talked about the significance of the play. He said: "It's really fascinating to have a look at some of Noël Coward's plays, particularly The Vortex, which caused a huge stir at the time, and see actually how important it was and how lucky we are to have it uncensored today."

While theatre censorship may have improved over the past 50 years, in the UK at least, other art forms continue to face oppression. Earlier this year Cuban artists Luis Manuel Otero Alcàntara and Yanelys Nuñez Levya, the winners of this year's Index on Censorship Freedom of Expression Awards for Arts, were refused a visa to the UK and missed the April ceremony.

The founders of The Museum of Dissidence – a public art project and website celebrating dissent in Cuba – fought a seven-month battle to gain entry into the UK and finally received their award in October at a ceremony held at Metal arts centre in Chalkwell Hall, Southend, where they were part of an artist-in-residence programme.

Alcàntara said artists "have a very important function. Like how the song of an artist can reach millions of people and make them cry, a picture from a visual artist can transform the feeling of what is happening in a country. This is something an artist has to take responsibility for".

In September Cuban authorities arrested Alcàntra and Nuñez for their roles in organising a concert against decree 349. Coming into force from 1 December, the law gives Cuba's ministry

> *We need to be vigilant about censorship which still happens today in the arts, both in the UK and abroad*

of culture increased powers to censor, issue fines and confiscate materials related to art they don't like. The pair say they were beaten whilst detained.

"Artistic expression in Cuba at this time is threatened by decree 349," said Index fellowships and advocacy officer Perla Hinojosa, who played a key role in campaigning for the activists' visas.

She said: "International recognition and bringing them here is important because it creates a wider audience for them and allows them to express the realities of what is happening in Cuba. It gives them credibility amongst authorities, and I am overwhelmed to experience their presence and know their strength coming from an environment that is very hostile. They are truly some of the bravest people I have ever met."

Another medium that Index have been covering recently is radio. Italian actor Marcello Mastroianni once spoke about his "devotion to an art form that evaporates" in reference to radio. Thanks to podcasting and digital databases, radio no longer has to evaporate and programmes can be downloaded and saved.

Editor Rachael Jolley recently visited Conversano in southern Italy to talk about the power of podcasts at an annual European cultural festival called Lector in Fabula. The trip tied into the theme of our autumn 2017 issue, which looked at ways in which radio is

gaining popularity at present and changing the news, cultural and information landscape. Several articles highlighted how podcasts are being used to smuggle information into authoritarian countries where news is tightly restricted.

"In some countries there aren't laws around what podcasts can do or how you can listen to them," Jolley said. "It's quite a clever and creative way of getting stories out to people who wouldn't necessarily be able to access them.

"Podcasting is being used in different kind of ways, but in another five years there might be something else, and in another 10 years →

ABOVE: (Top) Crowds visit cultural festival Lector in Fabula, Conversano, Italy; (Bottom, left) A group improvise at a theatre and censorship workshop at the British Library, London; (Bottom, right) Presentation of the Index 2018 fellowship to the founders of the Museum of Dissidence at Metal arts centre in Chalkwell Hall, Southend

ABOVE: Cuban artists Luis Manuel Otero Alcàntara and Yanelys Nuñez Levya with Index fellowships and advocacy officer Perla Hinojosa at Metal arts centre in Chalkwell Hall, Southend,UK

→ there might be something else. I think it's about how media evolves and how people get access to information in different ways."

Index head of advocacy Joy Hyvarian attended the first ever Cartooning Global Forum, which took place at Unesco's headquarters in Paris in October. The event brought together more than 70 cartoonists and supporters from all over the world to discuss issues such as peace, justice, development and the challenges that cartoonists are facing.

Participants at the Cartooning Global Forum included Cartoonists' Rights Network International, the free expression network IFEX, cartoonists such as Zunar from Malaysia and many others, including people who lost loved ones in the attack on Charlie Hebdo in 2015.

"Index believes that cartoonists should be celebrated as important contributors to democracy, but many governments fear the power of cartoonists," said Hyvarian.

"Governments censor cartoonists, persecute them and jail them. Earlier this year Index was part of a successful campaign to free cartoonist Ramón Esono Ebalé, who was jailed in Equatorial Guinea."

Ebalé's cartoons lambasted Teodoro Obiang, a dictator of nearly 40 years in Equatorial Guinea, for his deceit and corruption. His arrest caused a stir in the cartoonist community and after a global campaign, under the hashtag #FreeNseRamon, he was finally released in March after an officer admitted to arresting Ebalé on false charges.

Elsewhere, in the USA Index was involved in a meeting for the Global Network Initiative, a growing alliance of internet and telecommunications companies, academic institutions and human rights and press freedom groups. The organisation aims to challenge internet censorship. Index CEO Jodie Ginsberg also gave a talk in the Russell Senate building in Washington DC to discuss the Cloud Act (Clarifying Lawful Overseas Use of Data), a law which deals

with how the US government requests data from companies based in other countries.

At a conference held in Brisbane, Australia, Ginsberg was involved in debates and discussions surrounding some of the current greatest challenges in a divided world, such as how to approach arguments and how to be a better listener. Known as Integrity 20, the convention gathered journalists, artists and activists, amongst others. Ginsberg was involved in a heated roundtable discussing media ethics.

She said: "There's a lot of blame put on the media for the current world problems, you know, that the media have not behaved ethically, that the media just give a voice to extreme positions, which are valid criticisms, but I think to blame all of the problems on the messenger is a little bit of an overreach." ⊗

Lewis Jennings is the 2018 LJMU/ Tim Hetherington fellow at Index on Censorship

RIGHT: Actor Matthew Romain speaks at a Noël Coward-funded theatre and censorship workshop at the British Library in London

SUPPORT FREE SPEECH

Use your voice. Help those who can't.

AS WELL AS publishing a quarterly magazine, Index on Censorship is a non-profit that defends the rights of everyone to express themselves freely – no matter who or where they are. We work closely with artists and writers, and run an annual fellowship programme with specific support for four award winners. We rely entirely on the support of donors and readers to do this..

We can't do our work without your help, please do make a one-off or regular donation if you can.

END NOTE

The new "civil service" trolls who aim to distract

A new generation of trolls are officially employed by governments, with the Chinese government employing up to two million. **Jemimah Steinfeld** reports on the new global trend

47(04): 102/104 | DOI: 10.1177/0306422018819361

VITALY BESPALOV BECAME a Russian troll because he had lost his job in St Petersburg and was short of money. A journalist by trade, he was searching for content management jobs.

"One job announcement happened to be a job in a troll factory, but there were no descriptions of the kind of work I was going to do," he told Index.

At the time, says Bespalov, there was no information in the Russian media about troll factories. But it didn't take long for him to figure out the real nature of the work and he realised there was material there for a story. This was in 2014 and he worked in a department dedicated to creating disinformation related to Ukraine, from a pro-Russia stance, as well as in a troll department. There he would post several hundred messages a day.

The office where he was – pretty from the outside but like a "poor Russian hospital inside" – had around 200 employees. His boss, aged 30, had previously worked as a journalist. Bespalov thought she didn't like her job, but as time went on he saw she was "very involved". Most people, though, were "normal". They were young and, like him, attracted to the money (paid in cash, tax-free and better than the average St Petersburg salary).

Bespalov's story is far from unusual. But what is new in 2018 is that these people are now going on the state payroll. What's new is a recent Freedom of the Net report from Freedom House showed a significant rise in the number of governments using "paid pro-government commentators" to shape opinion online. Authoritarian governments have realised that if you can't beat them, join them; namely, if activists are going to launch revolutions and social movements via social media, so too will autocrats – and they'll make it financially enticing.

Recent Harvard University research from Gary King, Jennifer Pan and Margaret E Roberts analysed that the Chinese government's aim was to distract the public and ignore controversial issues. These people are known as *wu mao,* or 50 cent party members, because they are rumoured to be paid 50 renminbi cents per pro-China post. When the groundbreaking Harvard study investigated China's *wu mao,* it found that the people who were creating the social media posts were government employees of all ages and backgrounds. China leads the world here, employing millions of people with this in their job description.

"It actually makes sense," King told Index. "The Chinese government fabricates nearly 450 million social media posts each year, so it's a really hard management task. They already have millions of people working for them and these people flood sites such as Sina Weibo (one of China's biggest social media platforms) with government propaganda. Their tactic? To enlist civil servants. they just give them one extra thing to do.

Their tactic? To enlist civil servants, they just give them one extra thing to do

"These 50 cent party workers [are] not arguing against people arguing against the government. They're cheerleading. They are filling the internet with drivel." In his report, King labels this "strategic distraction".

Meanwhile in poverty-stricken Venezuela, a leaked government report from 2017 revealed plans for a project to set up a troll army with a military structure. One of its recruitment tactics is to reward people, who sign up to run Twitter and Instagram accounts, with food coupons, the value of which go up according to how much people post, and where. In Mexico, one troll told internet activist and journalist Alberto Escorcia that he had been paid 50,000 pesos (around $2,500) an hour to run up to 150 accounts against Mexico's #YaMeCansé [Enough, I'm tired] protests, which swept the country in the wake of the disappearance of 43 students in 2014; another hacker, Andrés Sepúlveda, boasted publicly that Mexico's government paid him more than half a million US dollars to help secure Peña Nieto's victory, using 30,000 Twitter bots.

India's social media is also awash with information spread by trolls. Swati Chaturvedi, journalist and author of I Am a Troll: Inside the Secret World of the BJP's Digital Army, has met several people who work in the industry. She told Index that the typical troll was motivated by money "because there is a huge unemployment crisis in India, and if you have an education there are not that many job opportunities".

"It's like what Hannah Arendt says in the Banality of Evil," she added. "They were

Proyecto de Formación del

EJÉRCITO DE TROLLS VENEZUELA

PARA ENFRENTAR GUERRA MEDIÁTICA

extremely ordinary people, they were like call centre workers. Only their job was to spew hate and abuse and make threats all day."

At the same time, Chaturvedi said a lot of them were "driven by the BJP's propaganda against minorities. They have a strange kind of persecution complex, which the [right wing Bharatiya Janata Party] is eating into". Their motivations are "a mix of ideology, where they really don't like minorities – they're very →

ABOVE: A leaked Venezualan government report from 2017 called A Troll Army Training Project to Confront the Media War

Through creating huge and largely loyal armies, government-sponsored trolls have driven many journalists into exile

→ anti-Islamic – and also the fact they they're paid well".

A report released this summer by California's Institute for the Future, State-sponsored Trolling: How Governments are Deploying Disinformation as Part of Broader Digital Harassment Campaigns, used a similar term – "information abundance".

"States have shifted from seeking to curtail online activity to attempting to profit from it, motivated by a realisation that the data individuals create and disseminate online itself constitutes information translatable into power," it said.

The report also says how state-sponsored trolling attacks in many countries "have grown out of, or been built upon, infrastructure and mechanisms established during election campaigns. Candidates and parties develop resources such as databases of supporters, committed campaign volunteers, social-media-influencing arms, and dedicated communications channels that are deployed during elections to advance a party's platform and undermine the opposition". They then use similar tactics and people once they're in power.

Rodrigo Duterte, Philippines' president, admitted to paying trolls during his election campaign. He denied using them once in office, but various media outlets have linked accounts used during his election campaign to ones which were active afterwards. The Duterte government "has even elevated bloggers and social media influencers acting as trolls to positions within the government", said the Institute for the Future report.

The efforts are successful. Through creating huge and largely loyal armies, government-sponsored trolls have driven many journalists into exile and silenced – or drowned out – other forms of online expression.

For Evgenia Sokolovskaya, a reporter for Snob Media, Russian trolls are a part of her day-to-day job. "Basically, each time we write about a sensitive topic, like criticising [President Vladimir] Putin and other politicians who are in Putin's favour, there are lots of trolls on social media," she told Index.

"They're always very angry, always trying to accuse everyone of everything."

Sokolovskaya usually brushes off trolls herself, but says it becomes more problematic for Snob's readers, when they are harassed. "Maybe some readers who don't understand what is going on might believe them," she said.

Chaturvedi says she gets, on average, about 10 to 12 death threats and rape threats a day. "But I know it's a call centre of hate. They have a hit list of journalists they want to attack," she said, showing a determination not to be intimidated. "In a weird kind of way there's nothing personal about it."

Does Chaturvedi believe the trend will get better? Indian Prime Minister Narendra Modi's troll army has already increased threefold in the lead up to next year's general elections, she says. "Unfortunately, the genie has been uncorked and I don't think [it] can be put back in the bottle." ⊗

Jemimah Steinfeld *is a deputy editor at Index on Censorship*

CORRECTIONS

|||||||||||||||||||||||||||||||||||||

ISSUE 47, THE AGE OF UNREASON, PAGES 4 AND 32

The sub-heading on p32 was incorrect and updated online to: Neuroscientist Clive Coen talks to Tess Woodcraft about why some people preserve their bodies after death, and the public's reaction to forecasting. The sub-heading for the same story on p4 was updated to: Dip into a discussion about why information works best for healthy democracies.